Dividend Stocks

Tony Pow

Why you invest

You need to learn about investing sooner or later in your life. You need to take some calculated risks.

Compare the returns of the following assets: cash, CDs, treasury bills, bonds, real estate and stocks. We start with the risk-free investments and end with the riskiest. It turns out that the average returns are in the opposite order. Cash and CDs are not risk-free as inflation eats our profits. For example, the real return is negative for the 2% return in a CD and a 3% inflation rate. In addition you have to pay taxes for the 'returns'. <u>Our capitalist system punishes us for not taking risk</u>.

There are two kinds of risk: blind risk and calculated risk. If you buy a stock due to a recommendation from a commentator on TV or a tip, most likely you are taking a blind risk. It would be the same in buying a house without thoroughly evaluating the house and its neighborhood. When you buy stocks with a proven strategy (i.e. when/what stocks to buy and when/what stocks to sell), you are taking a calculated risk. In the long run, stocks with calculated and educated risks are profitable.

Be a turtle investor by investing in value stocks and holding for longer time periods (a year or more). "Buy and Monitor" is better an approach than "Buy and Hold" as some could lose all the stock values such as in the failure of Enron.

For experienced investors, shorting, short-term trading and covered calls would make you good profits. Simple market timing would reduce your losses during market down turns. If you buy a market ETF and use my simple market timing, you should have beaten the market by a wide margin from 2000 to 2019.

With so many frauds and poor management, do not trust anyone with your investing. Do not buy investing instruments that are highly marketed such as annuity and term insurance.

If you are a handy man and do not mind to satisfy the constant requests of your tenants, buy real estate in growing areas could be very profitable in the long run. Take advantage of the tax laws such as investing in a 401K especially the part that is matched by your company and/or a Roth IRA.

Why you want to read this book

It should improve your financial health substantially in the long run.

- A best seller was written by a young writer whose main income was from his books and none from his investing. His book is good for beginners or you want to brush up your English. My major income is from investing.

- Most books on this topic do not consider cash or money market fund as a sector. The average loss in the last two market plunges is about 45%. When the market is plunging, cash is the best investment. Chapter 3 shows you how to spot market plunging.

- I select proven ideas from more than 100 books besides my original ideas and experiences. I also include links to current articles that will bring more depth to the topic. It is not a novel or documenting the story of my life. All related chapters are grouped in a section for easy future reference. Some chapters are not easy to digest as they have a lot of pointers and some may require you to try them out yourself.

- Many popular books claiming the authors making millions. However, usually their techniques are hard to follow. Many even admitted they had been bankrupted many times. Hence, their chance of bankrupting again is very high. Is bankruptcy fine with you? I cannot afford bankruptcy past and present. My techniques minimize the risk in investing.

- Pow P/E considers debt and cash for better prediction on the appreciation potential.

- This book has about 200 pages (6*9) and I do not waste your time in narrating the story of my life. Many 100-page books could turn into just a few pages of useful information after the narrating the story of the author's life.

- Check out my success stories.
  http://tonyp4idea.blogspot.com/2015/09/successes.html

My motivation to write this book is sharing my experiences, both bad and good. I provide simple-to-follow techniques using the free (or low-cost) resources available to us. I have been successful in investing for decades. I am enjoying a comfortable financial life. I do not hold back my 'secrets' as my children are not interested in investing. It is my small legacy in sharing my investing ideas.

If you are looking how to make 100% return overnight, there are many other books claiming to do so and this book is not for you and many books written by authors who have never make money in the stock market. Ensure those books that are readable but only have a few pages specific on the topic. This book describes how to be a 'turtle' investor making fortune gradually and surely.

As everything in life, there is no guarantee this book will make you money. However, the chance of success will be substantially improved especially when you practice on most of the ideas presented in this book.

My articles in SeekingAlpha.com.
Click the link (http://seekingalpha.com/author/tony-pow/articles).

Amazing returns

Amazing Returns

To achieve a consistent 10% return above S&P 500 over many years is every fund manager's dream. To double one's investment above the S&P500 return is amazing while tripling it is unheard of. I beat the S&P500 by 700% and I can detail the history of my transactions.

Many analysts show their average yearly returns and/or their returns of their top 10 stocks this time of year. The market has closed early today on Christmas Eve, so I have the time to check my recent performance. As a trader with many trades, it would be far too complicated for me to do the same for the entire year. I selected all the stocks I purchased in the last 90 days. Most of them are deeply-valued stocks. Let's check how I performed so far on these stocks.

Whenever you have achieved a high return such as this one, take the profit as it may have reached its peaks. To me, most profits are made in swing trades with an average holding period of just 90 days.

Stocks bought and their returns as of 12/25/12

Stocks	Date Bought	Return	SPY Return
BANR	12/07/12	3%	-.13%
KTCC	12/06/12	0%	.7%
QCOR	12/07/12	15%	-.1%
KTCC	12/06/12	-1%	.7%
ACTV	12/05/12	-5%	.7%
IAG	12/05/12	-1%	.7%
ADES	12/04/12	6%	.6%
NC	12/03/12	15%	-.3%
VELT	12/03/12	64%	-.3%
ANR	11/28/12	33%	4.8%
AAPL	11/16/12	1%	4.8%
C	11/14/12	13%	3.0%
DECK	11/13/12	16%	2.7%
MSFT	11/13/12	0%	2.7%
ALU	11/13/12	38%	2.7%
DLTR	11/09/12	7%	3.4%
CAT	11/08/12	4%	1.9%
MSFT	11/07/12	-8%	.5%
BSX	10/24/12	14%	.3%
BSX	10/19/12	7%	.3%

20			
AVG:		11%	1.35%

Beat SPY (in %) = (11%-1.35%)/1.35% = 716% or 7 times

Average Return = averaging each return of 20 stocks = 11%
Average Annualized Return = 148% or 122% (= 11% *365 / avg. holding period)
Average Return = Profit / Capitalization = 10%[1]

How the returns are calculated

Using BANR to illustrate how the return and the SPY return are calculated.

BANR	12/07/12	3%	-.13%

BANR was bought on 12/07/12 (17 days from 12/24/12) at 27.93 and it was at 30.43 on 12/24/12.
Rate of Return = (30.43 – 27.93) / 27.93 = 3%

SPY was at 142.53 on 12/07/12 and at 142.35 on 12/24/12.
  Rate of Return = (142.35-142.53) / 142.53 = -.13%

Commissions and dividends are not included for simplicity. Commissions are negligible and dividends could add about another 2% for the annual returns.

Interpreting the performance results

The quantity of each stock bought is not important as I am comparing the return of the stock. However, a few stocks have been listed twice as I bought two times usually on separate dates. If I chose them as one purchase instead of two, my return would appear even better. The purchases are real, so the amount of each stock is not identical to each other.

I'm not too excited yet. This phenomenal return could be just this one time only. 90 days is a short period. Consistency could be achieved with an improved stock picking technique, plain luck or a combination. By any measure, it is an extremely decent return. However, I do not expect beating S&P 500 by 7 times again.

My best return is from 2009 in my largest taxable account. It was over 80% beating the SPY by about 3 times. 2003 is another good year for profit. These two years are defined by me as the Early Recovery stage in a market cycle and the market provides the best profit opportunity.

The four losers are MSFT (-8%), ACTV (-5%), KTCC (-1%) and IAG (-1%). The best winners are: VELT (64%), ALU (38%), ANR (33%) and QCOR (19%). The following are in a 14% to 16% range: DECK, NC and BSX (2 purchases). Click here for the entire list.

Cheating the results

I could 'cheat' for better results by doing the following, but I did not:

1. Exclude stocks only purchased in last 20 days (instead of 15).

2. If my purchases of CSCO were included, the result would be even better. CSCO has been bought three times on 7/24/12 and it has gained 31% as of 12/25/12. I still have CSCO, but it is not included as it just hit the 90-days requirement.

3. I could include those buy orders that had not been executed due to their fast appreciation.

Hence, there are many ways to cheat, so you should read others' results carefully.

What stocks were included

There were 20 purchases. I bought some stocks twice and that counted as two purchases. None of the stocks have been sold as of 12/25/12. I have excluded the stocks that I am testing a strategy by trading them every month and most are in a separate account.

How the stocks were picked

The majority of the stocks were screened by my selected screens that had been proven profitable in the last 3 to 6 months, or are historically profitable at this stage of the market cycle. I also analyzed most of the screened stocks and assigned a score (15 and higher is a buy) based on the metrics that had a reliable predication recently. I do not stick with the scoring system 100% of the time, but most of them stocks that I purchased twice have high scores.

The poor performers were scored as: MSFT with a score of 13, ACTV 16, KTCC 27 and IAG 23. The scoring system is OK. MSFT should not be bought judging from its low score. However, I believe MSFT has a long-term appreciation potential. The other three are the latest purchases in this portfolio and they may perform better in a longer period of time.

The winners were scored as: VELT 34, ALU was not scored, ANR was not scored and QCOR 30. The scoring system is great for this group. ALU and ANR were selected from two Seeking Alpha articles and their selections were not based on these scores. I read several Wall Street Journal articles on ALU and CSCO to convince myself to buy both of them.

The average winners were scored as follows: DECK 9, NC 26 and BSX was not scored. DECK was selected based on an article from Seeking Alpha and it seemed DECK was experiencing the same short squeeze as CROX once did. BSX was selected from a Sunday paper article.

Observations

1. I notice that most big winners (ALU is $1) have a stock price less than $10. The myth of holding quality stocks with prices higher than $15 is not true here as most of my big winners were below $10 including ALU.

2. I did not double my normal purchases on VELT and ALU, which both turned out to be my best performers. VELT scored high in my analysis. ALU was very convincing but it seemed to be risky. 'Nothing risk and nothing gained' applies here. I did triple my purchase on CSCO, which is a large company with good fundamentals that were not yet 'discovered' by the market.

   Both AAPL and DECK gained more than 25% and then lost most of their gains during my short holding period. I should have sold AAPL as many of my fellow investors sold the winners expecting higher capital gains taxes next year. The myth of 'buy and hold' does not work here.

3. During this period, I had several buy orders that were not executed due to their rising stock prices. Market orders could be the solution. It is another example of pennies smart and a pound foolish.

4. It will be interesting to check the results again in 6 and 12 months. Except ALU, all are in my taxable accounts and I usually keep them for a year to qualify for the lower tax rates due to capital gains.

5. I have not described any specific method, but these concepts help you to build better strategies to customize to your individual situations and/or market conditions. Invest the money you can afford to lose. Past performance does not guarantee future results.

6. Reading articles such as Seeking Alpha can be beneficial providing they are not 'bump-and-switch' scheme. However, you should do your own analysis. It is your money after all.

7. The market has been up by .8% in the last 90 days and this portfolio increased by 11%. If my portfolio amplifies the market, I wonder whether it will be down by the same rate in a down market.

8. This portfolio is quite diversified even that I have not planned that way except weighing more with high tech companies. There are no big winners and no big losers that could change the average returns.

9. I tried not to include emerging countries such as China as I do not trust their balance sheets.

10. I have never achieved such an amazing return. I'm emotionally detached to big wins and big losses. It could be plain luck. Even the best strategy will have its "black swan" moment eventually.

11. To achieve over 100% annualized return is not sustainable by checking the top performers of the S&P 500 index and their returns. However, it is possible but not likely if you churn your portfolio more than once and you time the market correctly.

12. Time to take profits as most stocks here have achieved my objectives. Use the cash to buy stocks with a similar appreciation potential. You will never go broke taking profits.

Conclusion

My three steps of making a stock purchase are: 1. Market timing, 2. Screening stocks, 3. Stock Analysis and 4. When and what to sell. They have all been discussed throughout the book. Market timing and strategy (#2 and #3) does not always work, but it will go better with using them.

I am the living proof *against* the Efficiency Theory and the claims that stock picking does not work. It may not work from time to time, but in the long run it works.

Footnote

[1] Profit / Capitalization should be a little less than 20%. The original 10% is correct when you invest all the 20 stocks at the start of the beginning of the investment period. I bought these stocks on different dates. If I assume the average time of all the stock purchases is at a mid-point, then my average capitalization is only half and hence giving a 20% return.

It is slightly less than 20% as I did not include the stocks that I bought in the last 15 days. Use the number for a comparison and that's why we have to be concerned with the performance from most investment subscriptions.

Contents

Why you invest 2
Why you want to read this book 3
Amazing returns 5
Introduction 14
    Disclaimer 17
    Overview of Dividend Investing (by ChatGPT) 18
    1   The basics 20
    2   More on dividend stocks 25
    3   Potential problems 27
    4   Dividend growth 29
    5   Are dividend stocks better? 31
    6   Passive income 36
Dividends Screening 39
    1   Screening dividend stocks with Finviz 40
    2   Fidelity 42
    3   Sectors to be cautious with 44
Bonus Book: Evaluating Stocks 47
    1   A scoring system 48
Fundamental 53
Section I: Pick stocks for appreciation 53
    1   *Fundamental metrics* 54
        Mysteries of P/E 64
        Testing key metrics 71
    2   Finviz's parameters 74
        Your broker's website 82
        Other sources 82
        Gurus 83
        Quick and dirty 84
        5-minute stock evaluation 84

2	Finviz's parameters	86
	Your broker's website	93
	Other sources	93
	Gurus	94
	Quick and dirty	94
	5-minute stock evaluation	94
3	Intangibles	96
4	Qualitative analysis	100
5	Avoid bankrupting companies	104
6	Should you hold stocks forever?	106
7	*When to sell a stock*	108
8	Selling a winner	113
9	Examples of over-priced stocks	115
10	Technical analysis (TA)	116

Epilogue ... 121
Appendix 1 – All my books ... 122
    Best stocks to buy for 2025 ... 127
    Art of Investing ... 128
Appendix 2: Reviews by the unbiased AI ... 132
    Review of "Art of Investing 5th Edition " 9/10 ... 132
        ChatGPT Review ... 132
        DeepSeek Review ... 133
    Review of " Best stocks to buy for 2025" ... 136
    Review of "Sector Rotation 5th Edition" rated 9.5 ... 138
    Review of "Your first dollar for smart investing " ... 140
        ChatGPT ... 140
        Final Thoughts from DeepSeek: ... 141
    Review of "Momentum Investing 3rd Edition " ... 142
    Review of "Using profitable investment sites" rated 8 ... 143

    Review of "Investing successes and blunders" 144
Appendix 3 - Our window to the investing world 146
Appendix 4 - ETFs / Mutual Funds 146
Appendix 5 - Links 152

Introduction

This strategy is expected to be popular for the next 10 years or until the average CD rate beats the average dividend rate. We have a lot of retirees who depend on income from investments. The low interest rates from CDs and bonds drive these folks to dividend stocks.

Here is a simple screen to find these stocks. First find the stocks that have dividend rates more than 2% (about half of all S&P 500 stocks). Take out those sectors that give dividends as a return of equity (REITs and many partnerships). Eliminate the stocks with bad fundamentals such as high expected P/E (and earnings is negative), high debt (compared to companies in the same sector), etc. Next ensure that they have a good history of maintaining or increasing dividends (i.e. dividend growth).

As of 5-2014, it has been working well for the last five years. Be cautious on bank stocks, the drug companies, the miners and the insurers. I ignore foreign companies and ADRs (those foreign companies listed in the U.S. exchange). I prefer larger companies.

However, when a strategy is over-used, it may not work any longer. There may be a mild bubble on these dividend stocks due to too many followers. We will discuss how to protect our dividend portfolios.

In addition, we should not buy (actually should sell most stocks you own) stocks during a market plunge. Since 2000, we have two market plunges with an average loss of over 45%. We hope to have a maximum loss of 25% instead of 45%; most techniques depend on price movements and hence we cannot detect the peaks and bottoms. There are at least three variations on dividends:

1. Dividends given to stock owners (registered on and before the **ex-div date**).
2. Covered Calls. You can receive dividends while 'renting' your stocks.
3. DRIPs, Dividend Reinvest Plan.
http://en.wikipedia.org/wiki/Dividend_reinvestment_plan

How this book is organized

This book has 6 sections covering most areas in dividend trading.

Most graphs and tables are in landscape orientation for both paperback and e-readers. Some graphs may not be displayed adequately on a small screen of an e-reader. E-readers may be available in the current version of Windows, so you can read e-books on the larger screen of your PC. For better orientation, just flip the e-readers 90 degrees.

A link is usually included for these screens. Copy it to your browser to display the graphs on your PC if desirable. Instructions on how to produce some graphs are provided as you should try them out. One example is how to produce a chart on detecting market crashes.

It is easier to display some tables in landscape mode. Select a table or a graph via your e-reader to display it to fit the screen.

The font size and page size of most e-book formats can be adjusted. The unknown, special character is the "smiling face" that the current Kindle does not convert correctly as of this writing.

There are clickable links to web articles. Most of them are from my own web sites and public web sites such as Wikipedia. Some public links may not be available in the future as they are not under my control and my book offerings may change.

Fidelity Video provides video clips to explain some basic terms and it may require Fidelity customers to sign on in order to view them. Check the trial offer from Fidelity. YouTube offers similar video lessons.

These links extend the usefulness of this book by making available specific topics that may not be interesting to every reader. It also provides articles (most are not written by me) for more in-depth analyzes.

The current version provides most of the links the paperback readers can enter into your browser. Get the same information by entering a search in Wikipedia such as Dogs of Dow.

Investopedia is another source beside Wikipedia.
http://www.investopedia.com/

'Afterthoughts' includes my additional comments and comments from others. Readers can make comments in this book's website. These comments may be included in the Afterthoughts in subsequent revisions, with the commenter's last name redacted. It is the section of the article for freer and informal discussion. It also contains some political and social issues.

There are fillers with tips and jokes (most original) to fill up the empty space of the printed book. Fillers, links and afterthoughts may disrupt the flow of reading this book. However, no readers so far ask me to take them out.

For convenience, this book uses SPY, an Exchange Traded Fund (ETF) simulating the S&P 500, as the benchmark for the market.

Annualized returns (Return * 365 / (Days between)) are used where appropriate for more meaningful comparison. To illustrate, I have a 10% return in 6 months, a 10% in a year and a 10% in 2 years. It is more meaningful to use annualized returns of 20%, 10% and 5% respectively for the 6-month return, the one-year return and the 2-year return in this example.

Usually I do not include the dividend, so you can add an estimated 1.5% to the annualized return. In addition, compound interest is not used for easier calculation, so the actual return could be even better.

About the author

I graduated from Cal. State University at San Jose in Industrial Engineering and University of Mass. in Amherst with a MS in Industrial Engineering. My last job was in IT. I have been an investor for over 30 years.

Dedication

To all retail investors and future retail investors including my grandchildren.

I sincerely hope this book will build bridges with fellow investors with different backgrounds.

Important notices

© 2014-2023 Tony Pow: Email ID: pow_tony@yahoo.com

Version	Paperback	eBooks
1.0	12/14	12/14
2.0	11/16	11/16
3.0	10/19	10/19
3.4	11/21	02/23

Printed version.
ISBN-13: 978-1505246001 ISBN-10:1505246008

No part of this book can be reproduced in any form without the written approval of the author with the following exception.

Book store managers can order the printed books from Createspace.com.
https://tonyp4idea.blogspot.com/2020/12/book-managers.html

Book update.
https://ebmyth.blogspot.com/2020/12/updates-for-all-books.html

Disclaimer

Do not gamble money that you cannot afford to lose. Past performance is a guideline and is not necessarily indicative of future results. All information is believed to be accurate, but there it is not guaranteed. All the strategies including charts to detect market plunges described have no guarantee that they will make money and they may lose money. Do not trade without doing due diligence and be warned that most data would be obsolete. All my articles and the associated data are for informational and illustration purposes only. I'm not a professional investment counselor or a tax professional. Seek one before you make any investment decision. The above mentioned also applies for all other advice such as on accounting, taxes, health and any topic mentioned in this book. I am not a professional in any of these fields. Most of the time, I use annualized for better comparison; 5% in a month is more than 4% in a year for example. For simplicity, most of my returns do not include commissions, order spread and dividends. Same for all the links contained in this book. Some articles may offend some one or some organization unintentionally. If I did, I'm sorry about that. I am politically and religiously neutral. I try my best effort to ensure the accuracy of my articles. Data also from different sources was believed to be accurate. However, there is no guarantee that they are accurate and suitable for the current market conditions and /or your individual situations. My publisher and I are not liable for any damages in using this book.

Overview of Dividend Investing (by ChatGPT)

Dividend investing is a strategy that focuses on buying stocks that pay regular dividends—cash payments distributed by companies to shareholders. This approach allows investors to generate passive income while benefiting from potential stock price appreciation.

1. What Are Dividends?
A **dividend** is a portion of a company's profits paid to shareholders, usually on a **quarterly** or **annual** basis. Some companies also issue **special dividends** on occasion.

📌 **Types of Dividend Stocks:**
- **Dividend Aristocrats** – S&P 500 companies that have increased dividends for **25+ consecutive years** (e.g., Johnson & Johnson, Procter & Gamble).
- **Dividend Kings** – Companies with **50+ years of dividend increases** (e.g., Coca-Cola, 3M).
- **High-Yield Stocks** – Stocks that offer a **higher-than-average dividend yield**, often found in real estate (REITs), utilities, and energy sectors.

2. Key Metrics for Dividend Investing
- **Dividend Yield** = (Annual Dividend per Share / Stock Price) × 100
  - Example: A stock priced at $50 with a $2 dividend has a **4% dividend yield**.
- **Payout Ratio** = (Dividends Paid / Net Income) × 100
  - A **healthy payout ratio** is usually **30-60%**; too high (>80%) may indicate risk.
- **Dividend Growth Rate** – The **annual increase** in dividends over time.
- **Ex-Dividend Date** – Investors must own the stock before this date to receive the next dividend payment.

3. Pros & Cons of Dividend Investing
✓ **Advantages:**
☑ **Passive Income** – Steady cash flow, great for retirement.
☑ **Lower Risk** – Dividend-paying stocks are often more stable than growth stocks.
☑ **Compounding Growth** – Reinvesting dividends (via **Dividend Reinvestment Plans, DRIPs**) leads to exponential returns over time.

✅ **Inflation Hedge** – Many dividend stocks increase payouts over time, preserving purchasing power.

❌ **Risks:**

⚠ **Dividend Cuts** – Companies can reduce or eliminate dividends during financial trouble.

⚠ **Slower Growth** – Dividend stocks may underperform high-growth stocks in bull markets.

⚠ **Tax Implications** – Dividend income may be taxed at different rates, depending on classification (**qualified vs. ordinary dividends**).

4. How to Build a Dividend Portfolio

🔸 **Diversify Across Sectors** – Include dividend stocks from different industries (e.g., utilities, healthcare, consumer goods).

🔸 **Focus on Dividend Growth** – Choose companies with **consistent dividend increases** rather than just high yield.

🔸 **Reinvest Dividends** – Use **DRIPs** to compound your returns.

🔸 **Monitor Financial Health** – Check **payout ratios, earnings growth, and debt levels** to ensure sustainability.

5. Best Dividend Investing Strategies

1️⃣ **Dividend Growth Investing** – Focus on companies with consistent dividend increases (**Aristocrats, Kings**).

2️⃣ **High-Yield Investing** – Invest in **REITs, utilities, and energy stocks** for higher immediate income.

3️⃣ **Hybrid Approach** – Combine dividend growth stocks with high-yield stocks for **income and capital appreciation**.

6. Conclusion

Dividend investing is a reliable way to build wealth and passive income over time. It's best suited for **long-term investors** seeking financial stability and consistent returns.

1 The basics

Key Ratios for Dividend Stocks:

Ex-Dividend Date
To qualify for a dividend, you must own the stock on or before its ex-dividend date. Make sure to buy before this date if you want to receive the upcoming payment.

Payout Ratio
This ratio is calculated as dividends divided by profits. While a high payout ratio can look appealing, it also means the company is reinvesting less in research and development. Mature businesses often have higher payout ratios because they don't need as much reinvestment compared to growth-focused companies.

Companies can also return cash to shareholders through stock buybacks, which theoretically boost the share price:

> Earnings per share = Earnings / Outstanding Shares.

Reducing the number of shares can make earnings per share appear stronger, sometimes primarily to increase the value of management's stock options.

Dividend Yield
This is calculated as dividends divided by the share price.

Why Companies Pay Dividends
Companies have several options for using profits:
- reinvest in growth (R&D or acquisitions),
- buy back shares, or
- pay dividends to shareholders.

Ideally, management chooses whichever strategy most benefits investors. In practice, incentives often lead them to pick options that support the share price—and, by extension, the value of their own compensation packages.

Enhancements to Traditional Dividend Investing
Here are several practices I use to improve results:

Market Timing
I incorporate market timing into dividend investing. Sell most holdings ahead of a market downturn and repurchase when market indicators signal recovery.

Diversification
For portfolios under $1 million, hold around 10 stocks with no more than three in the same sector. For larger portfolios, consider holding 20 stocks. Too many holdings can dilute focus, while too few expose you to outsized losses from a single position. Adjust based on your experience and risk tolerance.

Stock Selection Criteria
Focus on stocks that meet these minimum thresholds:
- Share price over $2
- Average daily volume above 10,000 shares (or 8,000 shares if the price is over $20)
- Market cap over $200 million

In my experience, many of the biggest winners are priced between $2 and $15 and have market caps between $200 million and $800 million. These companies often fly under the radar of institutional investors. This is a guideline—modify it to suit your needs.

Country Risk
I avoid most small companies from emerging markets due to concerns about the reliability of their financial reporting.

Be Skeptical of Outlandish Claims
Ignore subscription services or books promising consistent returns over 30% or showcasing "5,000% gains." Such claims usually highlight winners while ignoring losers or rely on unrealistic backtests that exclude bankrupt companies ("survivorship bias").

If someone genuinely had a foolproof strategy, they likely wouldn't share it with strangers.

Remember, slow and steady wins. Investors who compound moderate gains over time often outperform those who swing for the fences.

Screening and Research

You can screen dividend stocks yourself or use reputable resources. Here are a few options:
- **TopYields:**
  Top Dividend Yields of Dividend Aristocrats
- **ETF Database:**
  High Yield Dividend Aristocrats Index ETF
- **Wikipedia:**
  S&P 500 Dividend Aristocrats

I prefer **Finviz.com** for screening—it's free, reliable, and also useful for market timing (using the 20-day and 50-day SMA).
Screening is only the first step. Once you have a shortlist, analyze each stock carefully.

Helpful Videos:
- Building a Dividend Portfolio:
  https://www.youtube.com/watch?v=ryN1aQxSefQ

- Best Dividend ETFs:
  https://www.youtube.com/watch?v=TPSw7On2gUo

- Dividend Investing Basics:
  https://www.youtube.com/watch?v=YBCmJU8osOo

- More Dividend Insights:
  https://www.youtube.com/watch?v=8B6WqiGhfvU

Additional Considerations
- **Taxes:**
  Consult a professional to understand how dividend tax rates apply to your situation.
- **High Yield Stocks:**
  Be wary of stocks with the top 25 highest yields—they often signal trouble or simply reflect yesterday's favorites. Instead, consider the next 25. Always confirm whether high yields stem from sustainable profits rather than return of capital.
- **Payout Ratios:**
  A payout ratio between 50–70% is generally healthy. Mature companies can support higher payouts.
- **Timing Anomalies:**
  Watch out for special dividends in Q4, such as in 2012, when companies paid extra ahead of anticipated tax increases.

- **REITs:**
  Remember that REITs must distribute at least 90% of earnings to maintain their tax status, and their dividends are taxed as ordinary income.
- **Buffett's Perspective:**
  Buffett on Dividends
- **Cash-Rich Companies:**
  Companies with substantial cash reserves and minimal dividends may later raise payouts, often boosting share prices.
- **Corporate Cash:**
  As of mid-2013, corporations held significant cash with relatively low debt, enabling higher dividends and buybacks amid a weak economy.
- **Dividend Grades:**
  Navellier Dividend Grader
- **Inspiration:**
  How a Janitor Built an $8M Dividend Fortune

Another Set of Dividend Criteria
- Yield over 2.5% (or at least 0.5% above the S&P 500 average)
- Dividend growth over the last 5 years (zero or better)
- Positive profit growth over the last 5 years
- Payout ratio below 70%
- P/E ratio under 25 with positive earnings
- ROE above 8%

If you can't find enough stocks that meet these criteria, dividend stocks may be overbought.

Other Income Sources
Beyond dividends, consider:
- Selling shares (mind tax implications)
- Buying bonds (favor high-rated bonds; avoid BBB and below)
- Investing in REITs and energy royalty trusts (note extra tax forms for taxable accounts)

#Filler: Let it DRIP, Dividend Reinvestment Plan

A DRIP, or Dividend Reinvestment Plan, automatically uses your dividends to purchase additional shares of the same company—often with no commissions and sometimes even at a 2–3% discount.

I've participated in several of these plans over the years. Over time, the shares accumulated through reinvested dividends ended up being worth more than my original investment. Just remember: when it comes time to sell, keep accurate records of your cost basis for tax purposes.

2   More on dividend stocks

- Check out the tax rate for dividends and the tax rate for your tax bracket with a qualified professional and act accordingly.

- It makes sense to evaluate more carefully the stocks with the top 25 dividend yield stocks. If the yield is that good, they could have some problems. It also could be yesterday's darlings. Try the next 25 according to an article I read. You need to further analyze each stock especially on the fundamentals. Ensure the high-dividend yields are not due to the return of capital as in some REITs and partnerships; it could be the reason why the top 25 dividend yield stocks do not perform.

- Use CCC charts by David Fish.
  http://dripinvesting.org/tools/tools.asp

- A good article on dividend stocks.
  (http://seekingalpha.com/article/1591272-the-7-habits-of-highly-effective-dividend-growth-investors?source=kizur)

- Check their payout ratios. When the company plows back most of its profit to dividends, the company will not grow as much. Many mature companies are fine in doing this. I prefer a payout ratio between 50-70%.

- Be careful in the last quarter such as in 2012 in identifying dividend and dividend growth stocks. It is a period when companies pay extra dividends expecting higher tax rates for their stockholders next year.

  REITs must pay out 90% of their earnings to maintain their REIT status. Their dividends are taxed as ordinary income.

- Buffett on dividends.
  (http://kinderflow.blogspot.com/2013/08/dividends-warren-buffett.html)

- Buy the companies that have a lot of cash and pay little or no dividends. There is a good chance these companies will pay dividends, or increase their dividends and the stock prices would usually appreciate.

- As of 7/2013, corporations had a lot of cash with low debt comparatively. Coupled with low interest rates and a weak economy, corporations increase their dividends and buy back their own stocks.

- Here is a site to grade dividend stocks.
  http://navelliergrowth.investorplace.com/dividend-grader/

- A successful story on dividend investing.
  http://finance.yahoo.com/news/heres-janitor-amassed-8m-fortune-234459317.html

- Here is another set of criteria for dividend stocks.
    - Dividend yield over 2.5% (or at least .5% above the average of dividend yield of all the S&P 500 stocks).
    - Dividend growth for the last 5 years is zero or higher.
    - Profit growth is positive for the last 5 years.
    - Dividend payout is under 70%.
    - P/E under 25 and earnings are positive.
    - ROE is over 8%.

  If you do not find too many of these stocks, the dividend stocks may be overbought.

- There are many other sources for income besides dividends:
    - You can sell some shares. Be sure to check out the tax consequences.
    - Buy bonds. Long-term bonds are favorable when the interest rates are high. Check the S&P bond rating. Forget the bonds rated BBB and below.
    - REITs and energy royalty trusts. Many require you to file extra forms if they are in taxable accounts.

Links

Building a portfolio: https://www.youtube.com/watch?v=ryN1aQxSefQ

https://www.youtube.com/watch?v=q3IG95iWwTU

3 Potential problems

When too many investors flock to a single strategy, it can create a bubble. One rare exception was the gold rally in 2010, driven by aggressive money printing after gold had been depressed for years.

There's a famous anecdote about a Wall Street veteran who sold all his stocks after hearing a shoe-shine boy boast about his stock picks—realizing it was pure herd behavior without any research behind it.

Similarly, when a TV reporter interviews someone like *Sarah Cohen*, who enthusiastically says she's investing in dividend stocks, it can be a modern "shoe-shine boy" moment—even if she's talented in other fields.

Massive inflows into dividend-focused ETFs signal this kind of mild bubble. Historically, retail investors often end up on the wrong side of the trade. For example, the flow of money into Fidelity's money market funds has at times served as a reliable contrarian signal.

Remember:
Past performance does not guarantee future results—especially when market conditions inevitably change.

Consider the early 2000s internet bust as an example of a widely loved strategy that failed spectacularly. As of 2015, dividend stocks arguably remain in a mild bubble. While they've outperformed the broader market, the margin isn't huge. Including troubled financial stocks like Lehman Brothers, AIG, and Bear Stearns in the analysis shows that dividend stocks have not always been safe havens.

Many analysts now argue that dividend stocks are overvalued, with their premium at the highest level in 30 years.

Consider Total Return
When evaluating any investment, think in terms of **total return**:

Total Return = Appreciation + Dividend + Covered Call (if used) - Taxes – Inflation

Institutional investors—the ones who really move markets—focus on total return. For their wealthy clients, capital appreciation is often more tax-efficient than dividends.

Capital gains give you more control over when taxes are paid. You can defer gains indefinitely in taxable accounts, and when you die, your heirs may benefit from a "step-up" in cost basis—potentially avoiding taxes on appreciation altogether. Dividends, on the other hand, are taxed as they're received.

For details on U.S. dividend tax rules, see: Dividend Tax – United States (Wikipedia) (http://en.wikipedia.org/wiki/Dividend_tax#United_States).

Afterthoughts

- Check the dividend performances and switch when they do not perform. http://seekingalpha.com/data/dividends
- Myths. http://money.usnews.com/money/blogs/the-smarter-mutual-fund-investor/2014/02/04/7-myths-about-dividend-paying-stocks
- From YouTube, Dividend stocks, dividend ETF https://www.youtube.com/watch?v=4kTnAJzp94k https://www.youtube.com/watch?v=OwLbsIWgcBs
- SA article in 2016. http://seekingalpha.com/article/3901726-fate-49-dividend-aristocrats-early-1990s-may-give-nightmares

Filler: Nightmare

Buffett called me—yes, *that* Buffett—and asked if I'd lead their stock research team. Stunned, I asked, "Why me? I'm a nobody."

He said he regretted not reading my book *Scoring Stocks* back in May 2013. Had he done so, he would've bought Apple instead of IBM, saving his firm millions—minus the $10 price of my book, of course. Not to mention the market timing method I shared that nailed the last two major downturns.
I told him, "Fine. I'll beat your fund's mediocre five-year return."

He replied, "At least beat the SPY. That way, investors won't feel so tempted to leave and trigger those nasty capital gains taxes."
I said, "That's tough. You *are* the market. Your size alone crushes any edge. My best trades? Small caps your fund couldn't touch without outright buying the company. Plus, good luck keeping day traders off my coattails."

Then I woke up, sweating. Thank goodness. Just a nightmare.

4 Dividend growth

The dividend growth strategy has performed well for many years, largely thanks to persistently low interest rates. With bond yields insufficient to support retirees' income needs, many have shifted toward stocks that pay reliable dividends. By 2015, however, this trend had pushed dividend-paying stocks to premium valuations. The question is: *When will it end?*

One way to monitor this is by comparing the performance of dividend-focused ETFs—like DVY—to broader market benchmarks such as SPY (which tracks the S&P 500). If these dividend ETFs begin consistently underperforming SPY over one- or three-month periods, it's often a warning sign that the mild bubble in high-dividend stocks is losing steam.

As of September 2015, many dividend ETFs had begun lagging behind the S&P 500. For those wanting to explore dividend-focused funds, here's a helpful resource:

Dividend ETFs_Dividend.com: (http://www.dividend.com/dividend-etfs/)

#Filler: QE

Quantitative Easing (QE) was designed to stimulate the economy, create jobs, and generate healthy inflation. But as of March 2015, it hasn't delivered those outcomes in most countries, including the United States.

A key problem: much of the cheap money hasn't flowed to the small businesses that drive job growth. Instead of relying on large banks to distribute these funds, it might have been better to channel more lending through the Small Business Administration (SBA). Meanwhile, large corporations have often used cheap capital for stock buybacks rather than productive investment—boosting share prices without necessarily creating real value. Consider this modified valuation formula: My PE = (Price − Cash + Debt) / Expected Earnings *(All values per share.)*

This adjusted metric accounts for a company's net debt position, providing a clearer picture of its underlying value. For even more precision, you can substitute "Net Current Assets" for "Cash," though this requires more detailed analysis.

QE's unintended effects also extend to the financial system. Big banks have funneled cheap money into margin lending for investors, helping drive the stock market to record highs and pushing margin debt to unprecedented levels. This dynamic has also contributed to widening the wealth gap, fueling social and economic inequality.

5   Are dividend stocks better?

There's an ongoing debate over whether dividend stocks or dividend-growth stocks outperform the broader market. My hope is that this section offers some clarity.

First, if you're already making money with your current strategy—stick with it. But from my own testing, I've found that dividend and dividend-growth stocks tend to underperform non-dividend stocks. If you're a dividend-focused investor, I encourage you to read this with an open mind.

On Testing and Bias
Be wary of forcing the data to fit your assumptions. Any test should be:
- **Reproducible** with identical results.
- **Free of cherry-picking** or selection bias.
- **Statistically meaningful**, with enough stocks and test runs to avoid random noise.

Below I describe the test procedure I used, which you can adapt to other strategies as well.

My Test Method
- **Stock selection:** Choose 30 stocks per category (Dividend Stocks, Dividend Growth Stocks, Non-Dividend Stocks, and All S&P 500 Stocks).
- **Timing:** Run 10 independent tests for each category, each starting at the beginning of a month and measuring the return over the following year.
- **Period:** Focus on the past 10 years to reflect recent market conditions.
- **Annualization:** Returns are annualized to standardize comparisons.
- **Universe:** Use the S&P 500. "All Stocks" includes all constituents, typically about 500 companies.
- **Dividend yields:** I estimated average yields to add to price returns—2% for the S&P 500, 5% for Dividend Stocks, and 4% for Dividend Growth Stocks.

(Note: Real-time dividend yields vary daily, so precise backtesting requires estimates or total-return indexes such as ^SP500TR.)
- **Definitions:**

- Dividend Growth Stocks: High yields plus dividend growth ≥ 10%.
- Non-Dividend Stocks: Selected randomly from S&P 500 stocks that pay no dividend.

You can cross-check these results against actual performance of dividend-focused ETFs and funds, comparing them to SPY (which tracks the S&P 500).

Why This Approach Matters

Unlike buy-and-hold fund marketing that advertises growth from a single $10,000 investment over 10 years, my "windowed" testing uses rolling one-year returns. This helps smooth out the effect of one spectacular or terrible year.

Also, note the danger of **survivor bias**—tests that exclude bankrupt stocks make results look better than reality. Many large firms that paid dividends have failed in the past.

Results

Here's a summary of my test results:

Category	Avg. One-Year Return	Beats All Stocks By
Dividend	10%	-1%
Dividend Growth	9%	-12%
Non-Dividend	16%	+62%
All Stocks	10%	N/A

Key takeaways:
- Dividend and dividend-growth stocks underperformed the average of all S&P 500 stocks.
- Non-dividend stocks dramatically outperformed, likely because they reinvest profits in growth or buybacks instead of paying them out.

I'll admit I was surprised by the magnitude of the difference.

Important Caveats

- Don't abandon your dividend strategy if it's working for you, especially if you use additional filters (e.g., ROE, low Price/Cash Flow, low Debt/Equity).
- This test is deliberately simple. Real-world portfolios can improve on these results with smarter screening.
- Be careful with small stocks in testing—they're more prone to bankruptcy, which creates survivor bias. My tests used the S&P 500 to reduce this risk.

Improving the Test

If you want to refine this kind of testing:
- Extend the rolling window to 12 months (creating ~120 tests over 10 years).
- Trim outliers (remove the single best and worst performer from each batch of 30).
- Weight recent years more heavily than older ones to reflect changing market conditions.

Survivor Bias Considerations

My historical database doesn't fully account for delisted stocks. When the S&P 500 has fewer than 500 entries in the data, it's often because failed companies were removed.
- Excluding bankruptcies like Lehman Brothers artificially boosts backtested results.
- Dividend stocks may have less survivor bias than non-dividend stocks, but I didn't adjust for that in my results.
- Ideally, you'd include delisted stocks to get the full picture.

A Quick Test: DVY vs. SPY

You can run a simpler test yourself by comparing DVY (a dividend ETF) to SPY:
- Add ~3% for DVY's estimated yield, ~2% for SPY's.
- In 2015, DVY returned -2%, while SPY returned +1%.
- Over the five years from 2011–2015, both averaged ~13–14% annually, showing roughly equal performance over that stretch.

A simple test

Compare DVY, a dividend ETF to SPY. Add 3% to DVY and 2% to SPY to include the estimated dividends. From the following table, 2015 was bad for dividend stocks but the performance for the last five years is about the same as SPY.

	Avg. Ann. DVY	SPY
2015	-2%	1%
1/2011-12/31/15	13%	14%

Summary

Dividend investing remains popular for income seekers, but don't assume it's automatically superior for total return. Always test your strategy carefully, avoid biases, and adapt to changing market conditions.

#Fillers: I wish I have a time machine

After collecting bottles for money, an old lady ordered a bowl of plain rice and ate by herself. I wish I could have ordered a meat dish for her and I was 'ashamed' of being generous.

A well-dressed gentleman offered his just-bought hamburger to a beggar. The beggar refused and asked for money instead – most likely he needed the money to buy liquor. A tale of two citizens.

During a lunch with my fellow tourists, a beautiful girl danced for our entertainment. I did not offer her anything and it had been bothering me for years.

During college, my housemates asked me to apply for food stamps. I had used only a few stamps then as I did not cook. I feel ashamed as this is my only time to collect social welfare.

We have regrets in life and we can only bring them to our graves.

#Filler

Teach the able welfare recipients how to fish instead of giving them fish for the rest of their lives. They will not work if you take out their welfare benefits for working.

Filler: Definitions of 'ism'

Capitalism is: You do not work, you die.
Communism is: Everyone is paid the same, so there is no incentive to work harder.
Socialism: As Margaret said, when we have nothing more to give, we all go hungry like the USA is going to.

Idealism: There is no such word in reality. It only exists in our dreams. However, many treat this as it is a reality as they're still dreaming.
Feudalism. Like the Tibetan monks in the 50s. Only the monks can learn and the rest are slaves.

6 Passive income

One of the main limitations of dividend stocks is that they're typically found in mature industries. As a result, their share prices often grow more slowly than the broader market. Personally, I also prefer the more favorable tax treatment of long-term capital gains.

If you see a stock offering an unusually high dividend yield, make sure to investigate *why*. It might be a warning sign rather than an opportunity.

Beyond individual dividend-paying stocks, there are many other options for generating passive income, including specialized ETFs:

REITs (Real Estate Investment Trusts)
REITs invest in real estate and distribute most of their income to investors—by law, they must pay out at least 90% of their taxable profits as dividends. Unlike buying and managing properties directly, investing in a REIT is similar to owning shares in a mutual fund that holds real estate assets.

As of 2022, I'm cautious about certain sectors within REITs. For example:
- **Malls**: Threatened by the shift to online retail.
- **Corporate offices**: Facing reduced demand due to remote work trends.

Corporate Bonds
Another source of passive income is corporate bonds, which you can access directly or through ETFs and mutual funds.
- I generally favor **investment-grade bonds** over junk bonds, especially in uncertain markets or when there's risk of a downturn.
- Be aware that **bond prices typically fall when interest rates rise**, since newly issued bonds will offer higher yields.

Links
REIT. https://www.investopedia.com/articles/04/030304.asp
Best dividend ETF: https://www.youtube.com/watch?v=TPSw7On2gUo
Passive income: Buy These 5 Assets To Replace Your Paycheck & Never Work Again

#Filler: Only in California

I was once robbed of $1,000. Strangely enough, the robber handed me back $50 and even helped me call the police. Turns out, in California, theft under $950 isn't prosecuted as a felony—so the police have "more important" crimes to focus on. It makes you wonder if the law was written by lobbyists for the criminals. Like they say: you've got to spend money to make money—even in crime.

Dividends Screening

Besides screening dividend stocks yourself, there are many sites providing this information. You can google 'dividend stocks'. The following are some of them.

TopYields
http://www.topyields.nl/Top-dividend-yields-of-Dividend-Aristocrats.php
An ETF on Dividend Aristocrats
http://etfdb.com/index/sp-high-yield-dividend-aristocrats-index/

From Wikipedia on S&P Dividend Aristocrats
http://en.wikipedia.org/wiki/S&P_500_Dividend_Aristocrats

There are many sites to screen dividend stocks. I select Finviz.com that should give us the best result and are free. In addition, we use the same site for market timing.

Screening is only the first step. Need to filter the good ones from the bad ones.

1   Screening dividend stocks with Finviz

You can use your screen from your broker or any site and then evaluate stocks using technical indicators (simpler than it looks).

Finviz.com provides a screening incorporating both fundamentals and technical metrics and it is one of the best free sites. Bring up Finviz.com in your browser and select screener. You have 4 tabs: Descriptive, Fundamental, Technical and All.

Besides incorporating technical indicators, it has the following features:

- The criteria specified can be saved.
- The searched stocks can be saved in a portfolio (for paper trading and performance monitor).
- For extra fee, you can have historical database (I have not tested this feature to comment).
- Some advanced technical indicators such as Candlestick (very useful as a momentum indicator).

However, it lacks the following features:

- Stocks with prices trending up in the last several weeks (such as increasing X% in previous week and y% in week before the previous week, etc.).
- Using exponential moving averages that have better predictive power than simple moving averages for momentum investing.
- Selecting ranges (for example, it cannot select all three major exchanges, market cap ranges, etc.).

Screen Criteria

The screen parameters (i.e. selection criteria) are briefly described here. They are guidelines. Adjust them to fit your risk tolerance and requirements. Monitor them from time to time as the market always changes. If you have too many stocks, restrict your criteria. If you have too few stocks, relax them.

As of 5/2014, I found 12 stocks that satisfy the above criteria.

In addition, they should be in one of the 3 major exchanges: NYEX, NASDQA and AMEX – Finviz.com allows you to select one exchange at one time. Avoid most foreign stocks that may charge extra fees.

Finviz.com does not indicate dividend growth. Prefer positive dividend growth for the last 3 years (some prefer 5 years). Ensure dividend yield (dividend / stock price) is not a result of decreasing stock price. When your stock is bankrupting, the dividend yield based on past dividend would be astronomical!

Click P/E to sort with the lowest P/E first but avoid stocks with negative earnings (from P/E). If you prefer dividend over P/E, select the stocks with high dividends.

The next step is to evaluate fundamental sound stocks in next section.

I recommend to paper trade your strategy using different selection criteria. When you are comfortable, commit a small sum and increase your portfolio size gradually.

Here are three articles on using Finviz.com's screener.

Investopedia.
http://www.investopedia.com/university/features-of-Finviz-elite/other-chart-features.asp
How to scan using Finviz (YouTube).
https://www.youtube.com/watch?v=aQ_0FTg9Cfw
Screening using technical indicators.
https://www.youtube.com/watch?v=RZRP2NeSX0s

Dividend stocks

The list changes almost every quarter as their fundamentals, the market and the sector change. Most are mature companies that do not have to plow back money for research and development. The following is a sample list:

AAPL, AAR, ALV, CLX, ERF, HP, JPM, KMB, MAT, MCD, PEP, PGH, PM, WMT, WFC and XOM. In addition, you can buy an ETF (DVY, SDY, VIG…) with high dividend yields or a mutual fund (FRDPX).

2   Fidelity

Fidelity offers a strong screen function. The most unique feature is incorporating its Equity Summary Score (used to be Analyst's Opinion) and some outside researches such as Zacks and Ford.

From the main menu, select "News and Research", "Screen and Filter" and then "Start a screen". The following example selects stocks with the following criteria: Security Price (2 to 250), Market Cap. (300 and above), Equity Summary Score (8 and above), Zacks (Strongest) and Ford (Strongest).

It displays the 10 stocks. Research each stock. Read the News about each stock. You may want to use Finviz.com, Yahoo!Finance and other sources to double check.

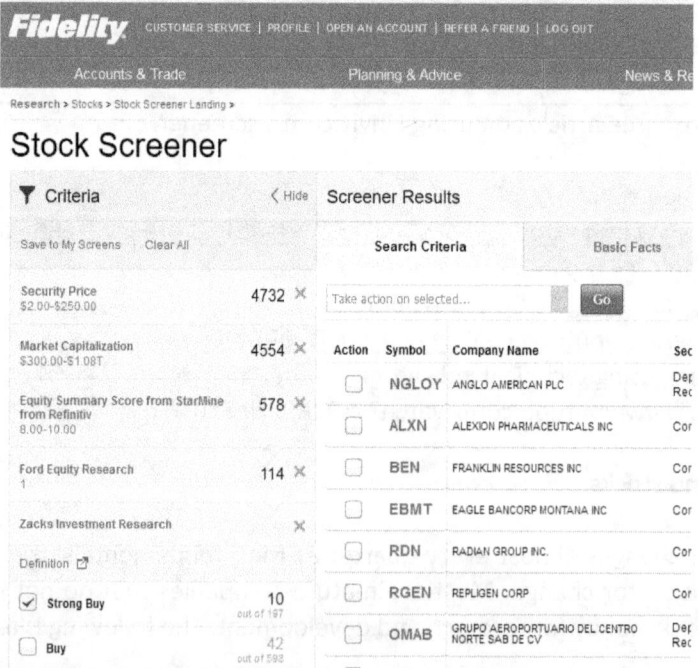

The following describes some of the features.

- Equity Summary Score. It is one of the major metrics I use in my proprietary scoring systems. They are not available to many small stocks. From my limited database in 7/2015 and for short durations, the results are:

Short Term: (7% return for the average)

Metric	Parm. 1	No. of Stocks	%	Parm. 2	No.	%	Predictability
Fidelity Analyst	Buy	150	10%	Sell	279	3%	Good

Long Term: (8% return for the average)

Metric	Parm. 1	No. of Stocks	%	Parm. 2	No.	%	Predictability
Fidelity Analyst	Buy	90	17%	Sell	208	4%	Good

It has its own limits, but they are very minor to me.

First, it does not have a historical database for verifying the screen performance such as the return after a year. However, I do not know any site that provides this function free. To work around this, I save the results in a spread sheet and update the performance.

Secondly, it does not provide many other filter criteria that can be found in other systems such as technical indicators or insider transactions found in Finviz.com. I use other sites for further evaluation.

Most investors should find that this screening is a very good tool and very easy to use.

3   Sectors to be cautious with

There are many reasons to be very cautious when investing in the following sectors. However, Technical Analysis (a.k.a. charting) would give you more hints than the fundamentals for stocks for these sectors. If the big guys are dumping, most likely Technical Analysis (or the simplest SMA-20) would tell you that.

Loan companies/banks

The financial statements do not show the quality of their loan portfolios. Following this advice, you may be able to skip the banks that melted down in 2007. The peak of Citigroup is $550 and several banks went bankrupt.

Many metrics are not relevant for banks such as Debt/Equity and EBIT. The rising interest rate would be good for banks' profits.

Drug (generic is ok)

Understanding the complexities of the drug pipelines, its potential profits for new drugs and the expiration of the current drugs may not worth the effort for most retail investors. In addition, a serious lawsuit and / or a serious problem with a drug could wipe out a good percentage of the stock price. When a drug shows unpromising sign(s) in any trial phase, the stock could plunge and vice versa.

Miners

It is extremely difficult to estimate how much ore (sometimes a miner owns several different types of ores and/or of different grades in the same or different mines) that a company has. It is further complicated by the complexities to extract and transport them. When the total of these costs is greater than its production price, the company will not be profitable. Understanding the market for ore futures is another discipline.

Many mining companies are in foreign countries such as Canada, Australia and countries in South America. Their financial statements of Canada and Australia are more trustworthy than most other emerging countries.

One potential problem of mining companies from many emerging countries is nationalization.

Mining rare earth ore is extremely risky when the profit depends on how China, a major producer of these ores, will price these ores. After China announced the export restrictions on rare earth elements, several non-Chinese companies announced to reopen their mines for rare earths, but few have made any profits as of 2013. Developed countries have stricter environmental regulations.

Coal and eventually oil suffer from the rising use of cleaner energy such as solar and wind.

Insurance companies

Insurance companies profit by:

1. The difference between the total premiums received and the total claims minus expenses in running the company.

2. How well they invest the premiums; you pay your premiums earlier than you may collect from any claims.

They can protect the profits in #1 by restricting claims by natural disasters such as earthquakes and by re-insuring. However, a bad disaster could wipe out a lot of their profits.

Even if the insurance company shows you its investment portfolio, most of us, the retail investors, do not have the time and expertise to analyze it.

Emerging countries (not a sector)

Their financial statements especially from small companies cannot be trusted, and many countries use different accounting standards. Emerging countries are where the economic growth is. I trade FXI, an ETF, rather than individual Chinese companies. I have lost a lot in small Chinese companies due to frauds and politics. To check out whether the stock is an ADR, try ADR.COM (https://www.adr.com/).

Stocks with low volumes (not a sector)

Most likely you pay a high spread to trade these stocks. They can be manipulated easier. I had a hard time trying to sell a stock owned by a few owners.

For simplicity, I trade stocks with the average daily trade volume over 6,000 shares (double it if the price is $2 or less). A better way could be by calculating the percent of your trade quantity / average daily trade volume; it would reduce the effect of penny stocks that have larger volumes due to the low prices.

Good business and bad business

Banking is a good business in a growing economy. My deposit in them makes virtually zero interest, and they loan the same money making 3%. If they are more cautious in loaning, they should make good profits.

Restaurant is an easy business to run, but it is very hard to make good money. With the rising of minimal wages, it will get even tougher. That could be the reason for so many coupons today. The high-end restaurants are doing better due to the rising stock market. The pandemic of 2020 would wipe out a lot of small restaurants.

Retailing is a tough business. Look at the top 10 retailers 15 years ago, I can only find two including Macy's that are still surviving. Most are either went bankrupt or being acquired. Even Macy's was not in good financial shape. Amazon is the killer.

Airlines are a tough business. You can tell by the average increase in fares in the last 10 years. It cannot even beat inflation. They have to charge you for everything. The next frontier charge is the rest room (especially for long-distance flights). Now I understand why they call themselves "Frontier Air". As of 2014, it is quite profitable due to mergers and lower fuel cost. The pandemic of 2020 may be the toughest time for airlines. As of 5/2020, Boeing has many serious troubles and they can only survive with a bailout from the government.

There are several software companies that produce software such as the virus detecting programs and tax preparation software. The customers faithfully buy new versions every year. That's great business.

Bonus Book: Evaluating Stocks

The simple formula to make money is to find value stocks and wait for the market to realize their values; it could be a year away. Momentum investors buy stocks that are treading up, and evaluate the purchased stocks again within 3 months. Personally I sell within a month as usually there are better momentum stocks to buy. Only buy when the market is not risky. Aggressive investors find the worst stocks to short. Most successful investors are doing this.

The book value of a stock is simply the net worth of a company (= Assets – Liabilities). When the stock price is higher than the book value per share (i.e. 'Stock Price / Book Price' > 1), it is over-valued. When this ratio is more than 2 or less than 0.5, conservative investors have to be cautious. When it is way underpriced, there may be a critical reason.

Intrinsic Value includes the intangibles such as patents. However, both the Book Value and Intrinsic Value have not been convincing predictors from my tests. I briefly describe some basic but important metrics here.

- Expected (same as Forward) Earnings Yield (E/P). The future appreciation depends on future earnings and the current price of the stock (you do not want to overpay). I prefer a range from 5% to 30%.
- Growth of Earnings and growth of sales. Compare them to their numbers in the same quarter of last year. I prefer 10% or higher.
- How good is the management? It is measured by ROE. I prefer 10% or higher.
- How safe is the company? 'Debt/Equity' is one important metric and Cash Flow is another. The warning sign is that the company does not have enough cash to pay back the debt obligations. I prefer it is less than .5 (same as 50%). However, some industries are debt-intensive.

Most ratios are readily available from many sites including Finviz.com. In most cases there is no need to dig into the complicated financial statements initially. If you do, ensure they are up-to-date. For example, when a stock has a one-to-two split, the price is updated but may not be the Earnings per share, Book per share, etc.

The predictability of most metrics changes according to the current market conditions. Monitor their performance and act accordingly.

How to start

First we filter stocks from about 7,000 selected stocks available from Finviz.com for example; the number is variable from different web sites and/or services. To start with, skip stocks that are not in the three major exchanges, market caps less than 50 M, or daily average volumes less than 10,000 shares.

Check out the "Simplest Way to Evaluate Stocks" in the Common Tools section to evaluate stocks for beginners and couch potatoes. Furthermore, refer to Scoring Stocks to evaluate stocks via a scoring system.

1   A scoring system

This scoring system helps you to select whether you should buy a stock or not. In this system, when a stock scores higher than 2, it is a buy. As a group, the highly-scored stocks usually perform better than the lowly-scored stocks in a year. The basic concepts are described here.

An Example

For illustration purposes, we use two metrics: Forward P/E and ROI.

First we convert Forward P/E into Forward E/P by flipping the two values. Assuming Forward E/P should have a higher weight than ROI, multiply E/P by 5. The average ROI is 10% (simplified for illustration), so minus it by .1.

Score = Forward E/P * 5 + (ROI -.1)

For example, a stock has a P/E of 10 (E/P = 1/10= .1) and ROI is expressed as 25%.

Score = .1 * 5 + (.25 - .1) = .5 + .15= .65

Some parameters by some sites are expressed in grade such as A, B, C and D. For simplicity, if it is A, then the value is 2 otherwise it is zero.

Score = if (Grade = "A", 2, 0) + ...

Test your system on paper with at least 3 months of data. Check whether your scoring system works. It works when the higher the score corresponds to the better the return. Adjust the weight on each metric and see whether your scoring system improves its predictability.

Again, it is simplified for educational and illustration purpose. Try even more different metrics and check whether the metrics still work in the current market. The next metrics to include could be Equity Summary Score from Fidelity, Debt/Equity and Quarter-to-Quarter Earnings / Sales.

Monitor your scoring system

I am sure that many have tried to use most of the metrics and they still cannot find the Holy Grail. I believe the predictability power of each metric is influenced by the current market conditions. For example, the fundamental metrics such as P/E predict better than the growth metrics such as PEG during the market bottom. You should test the performance of each metric every 6 months or so.

You may have two scores: one for short term and one for long term. The stocks you want to keep in the short term may not be the same kind of stocks you want to keep in the longer term. Short term is 3 months (one month for me) and long term is 12 months for me. My definitions could be different than yours. Value metrics are more important for the long term while growth metrics are more important for the short term.

However, 12 months is too long a period of time and during this period the market may change, so it is better to change it from 12 to 6. To illustrate, energy stocks were great in 2007, but they plunged in 2008. If your scoring system for long-term holding was constructed based on 12 months' data in 2007, the system would have been misleading in 2008 for energy stocks in this example.

I find the short-term scores have a better prediction power than the long-term scores. However, I keep profitable stocks more than 12 months to qualify for the better tax treatments in taxable accounts, and sell the losers less than 12 months. Evaluate the purchased stocks every 6 months to decide whether you want to keep them for another 6 months. Use stops and trialing stops (for winners) to protect your portfolio.

Besides monitoring the metrics in your scoring system, monitor the scores.

The market is not always rational
Sometimes the scoring system fails: When the poorly-scored stocks perform better than the highly-scored stocks. The market is not always rational. Most scoring systems depend on fundamental metrics. When the market switches its favor from value to growth, adjust the score system accordingly. I have found that more than one time that the stocks scored in the top 5% did not perform, so be careful or skip the top 5% (sometimes 10%). The events such as a pending lawsuit or an expiring drug do not show up in metrics, and that is why we need to do other analysis such as Intangible Analysis.

Some metrics almost always work such as the positive predictions of excessive insider's purchases. The insiders know the company typically better than others. When they buy their own company's stock at market prices, they must know it has good appreciation potential. They have many reasons to sell their company's stocks. However, when they sell a large percent of their holdings, be cautious.

When the stock loses more than 30% in a month and you cannot find valid reasons, it may be a good indicator for potential appreciation ahead. Some suggestions are:

- Do not modify your scoring system during market plunges.
- The best strategy is to use the screens (same as searches) that have worked well for the last 90 days.
- Find out why your fundamental metrics that used to work do not work now. You may want to add more weight on growth metrics, and vice versa on value metrics.

An example of monitoring the metrics

This is what I found in monitoring the performances of the metrics as of 3/2013. It is based on a limited database of about 300 stocks with holding periods varying from 1 to 15 months. It has an average of 8% (16% for shorter term). The following is for educational purpose only.

1. The foreign stocks are not doing well: South America (average return is -21% for 7 stocks), Israel (-18% for 2), China (-10% for 7). Europe (0% for 17) and Canada (5% for 16, and most are in natural resources). If I ignore the foreign companies, the return of the portfolio would be increased substantially.

2. The following metrics work fine for the long term only: Forward (same as Expected) Earnings Yield (E/P) and Fidelity's Equity Summary Score.

3. P/B. The stocks with P/B less than 1 perform better than the stocks with P/B greater than 2 (10% vs. 4%).

4. There are no definitive conclusions on Cash / Market Cap, PEG and Return of Equity (a surprise to me) in this monitor.

5. The stocks that were cheaper by 50% to their average 5-year P/E (available from Fidelity) have performed better than those stocks that were cheaper by less than 2%.

6. The ratio of Short / Market Cap between 25% and 30% has better performance than other percentages. It is a contradictory ratio and it could be a short squeeze (a condition that the stock is running out of shares to sell short).

7. There are many composite scores from different vendors that I subscribe to and they are not disclosed here.

8. Based on the above, I will modify my scoring system. I will still have two scores, one for short term and one for longer term.

Short-term scoring system

The scoring system should work better in the shorter term. For testing this system, I used the above data base, but deleted stocks that have been over 8 months old. It is still a small data base of about 190 stocks.

The result is different from the above as the time frame has been reduced. Here is the summary.

1. The predictability of screens (same as searches) performs about the same as the last monitor. A few screens are better than others. I will not use the under-performing screens with real money.

2. The stock grades from several vendors are not a good indicator this time.

3. Expected (same as Forward) Earnings Yield (E/P) has been a good indicator.

4. Cash Flow is a good indicator (different from the last monitor).

5. Fidelity's Equity Summary Score is a good indicator. Finviz has a similar score, but I prefer to use Fidelity's. Fidelity places higher weight on opinions from analysts that have a better prediction on this stock than others. It eliminates some of the conflict of interest between the analysts and the investing banks s/he works for.

6. The Short Percentage between 25 and 30 is a good contrary indicator (could be a good chance for a short squeeze).

   Its value of less than 10 % is a good indicator. The rest of the range is not conclusive.

7. Cash / Market Cap, Insider Purchase, P/B, ROE and Dividend stocks (>3%) are not conclusive in this monitor.

8. P/S with values less than 0.8 are a good indicator.

9. For some reason I do not know why and how to explain: the top 10% of the top-scored stocks did not perform better than the other stocks that pass.

   It happens in both my two scoring systems. Be suspicious of them and it has happened for more than once. However, the stocks that scored in the bottom 10% are consistently poor performers and that's a good indicator.

There are many other parameters that may be of interest to you. Include them in the performance monitor.

Fundamental

Section I: Pick stocks for appreciation

After the market is not risky (Section I) and we have picked up stocks (Section II), we still need to evaluate the stocks. Most stocks with bad fundamentals will not appreciate. However there are examples on turnaround situations (some call them catalysts) such as:

- A new drug has positive test result.
- A new product.
- A new discovery or breakthrough.
- Being acquired.
- Being settled with a major lawsuit.

Screen stocks first and then analyze the screened stocks one by one.

The most updated information is from the Earning Conference Call (easier to obtain it from SeekingAlpha), Q10 report and from the company's web site. Finviz.com seems to be more updated than most other sites besides the above.

When to sell a stock? I have three chapters at the end of this section. They are in the same topic but in different approaches / concepts.

The better analysis gives you better chance of success, but as everything in life there is no guarantee.

Myths on dividend stocks

- Dividend yield determines the value of a stock. Not true. Apple did not pay good dividend for a long while. Many financial stocks with great dividend yield bankrupted in 2008.

    How about borrow money to pay dividends?

- P/B is one of the 3 pillars (besides dividend yield and P/E). Not true as the book value does not contain intangibles that could worth a lot especially for established companies.

1 Fundamental metrics

ROE

Return of equity (ROE = Net Income / Equity) could be the most important financial indicator to determine how well the management is doing their job. However, in recent years, this metric has been overused and loses its prediction reliability.

The company's return on equity for at least the last five years would indicate how the stock price endures major financial downturns as well as upturns.

Comparing the ROE to the average ROE for the sector is a good indicator on how well the company is managed compared to its peers. Some sectors including utilities have low average ROEs.

Market Cap (Capitalization)
Market Cap = Total no. of outstanding shares * share price

I recommend the beginners buy U.S. stocks with a market cap greater than 800 M (million). Here are the current conventions (everyone's convention is different) and they should be adjusted to inflation.

Class	Market Cap (million)
Nano Cap	< $50M
Micro Cap	$50M to $250M
Small Cap	$250M to $1B (billion)
Mid Cap	$1B to $10B
Large Cap (Blue Chip)	$10B to $50B
Mega Cap	>50B

The higher the cap is, usually the less risky the stock would be. Nano Cap and Micro Cap are reserved for speculators or owners of the companies. Small Cap and Mid Cap are for knowledgeable investors as most institutional investors would skip these stocks in these caps especially Small Cap. Large Cap, Mega Cap and some Mid Cap are the stocks traded by institutional investors. They are thoroughly researched continuously.

My metrics

My current favorites are Forward P/E, PEG, Fidelity's Equity Summary Score, Short % of outstanding shares, Free Cash Flow, ROE and Debt Load / Equity.

In addition, I use many summarized metrics from different sources. For example, one of my subscription services gives me a composite rank for fundamentals and another one for momentum. To illustrate, click here for Blue Chip Growth which is no longer free for stock analysis. Enter IBM as the stock symbol. As of 2/2013, it gives C for a Total Grade, D for Quantity Grade and B for Fundamental Grade. The Total Grade is usually a composite grade of other grades.

Use the metrics to screen through the stocks to reduce the number of stocks for further consideration.

Mid, high and low values of common metrics

Metric	Mid Range	Low Range	High Range
P/E (last 12 months)	< 10	>40	< 4
Price / Cash Flow	< 12	>30	< 4
Price / Sales	< 2.5	>3	< .2
Price / Book	< 2.0	>4	< .2
PEG	< 1.5	>2	< .2

High Range means good values (although in this table it means low numbers), but sometimes it is too good to be true. Low Range means bad values. To illustrate, many internet stocks in 2000 had P/E over 40 (bad) while a neglected bargain stock has a P/E of 3 (supposed to be good). A bargain could also mean they could have some hidden problems. In reality, I prefer the Mid Range. Using P/E to illustrate, it should be between 4 and 10. Adjust the range according to your personal tolerance and the current market conditions. If the market trend is up, you may want to relax the range to 5 to 12 for example otherwise you cannot find too many stocks for further evaluation.

These values are my selections based on data for about 10 years. They are used for predicting the performance of a stock in a year; review the ranges every 6 months in the current market.

The metrics with the high-range and mid-range values offer better predictions for the stock price appreciation. From the above table, the stocks with the low-range values have a better chance than other stocks to lose money in a year or so. Some favorable numbers could be high values instead of low values such as ROE.

However, the range values could change. When the market favors momentum or you do not keep stocks for less than a month or so, the momentum metrics including PEG and price growth could be better predictors. We need to check to see whether the current market favors which metrics: Value or Growth – some websites and subscription services identify the current favorite. In addition, the performance of each metric should be evaluated every 3 to 6 months. In addition, new range values need to be adjusted with the above table.

Fundamental metrics take a longer time (about 6-12 months vs. 1 month for momentum metrics) for the performance to materialize. The metrics in the above table besides PEG are all fundamental metrics. Except for financial stocks, P/B is always worthless.

Examples of searching with high range values

Stocks with low-range values for most metrics (such as 40 in P/E in the above table) could be risky. Hence, select the stocks with the mid-range value (e.g., 10 for P/E). Avoid the low-range values indicated by the metrics.

Here is one example of selecting stocks with high range values of P/E and P/B. Most likely, you will not find too many stocks with these criteria.

$E > 0$ and
$P/E < 4$ and
$P/B < .2$

E is earning per share and we need the company to be profitable.

High range values could indicate something is wrong with the company, e.g., a lawsuit pending. I would consider a P/E of less than 4 is suspicious. However, very small companies are often neglected by the market, so they could be solid companies. Don't forget to do your due diligence and spend more time in thoroughly evaluating the stock and its industry.

The stocks with the low-range values have a greater chance of losing money in the next year or so. That is proven statistically as a group despite some exceptions. AMZN[2] is not a valued stock by its high P/E or its high P/B. However, if the company is investing for the future by building infrastructure and capturing the market share, you may ignore these unfavorable metrics. Personally, I prefer fundamentally sound companies today.

Note. P/B is not a good metric for established companies and / or companies with a lot of research such as IBM. Many metric formulae are outdated due to ignoring intellectual properties, patents and market appeals such as brand names.

Example of a search for mid-range values
E > 0 and
P/E < 10 and
P/E > 4

In this case, you only include companies with positive earnings and P/Es within the range from 4 to 10 exclusively. You should find many companies with the mid-range values of P/Es.

Add other filters such as minimum price, market cap and average volume. If you do not find too many stocks, relax your criteria (start with mid-range values in the table), and vice versa to limit the number of stocks. If you usually find stocks with a screen but not today, it usually means that the market is overvalued and that you cannot find many bargain stocks.

Again, it is the first step to narrow down the number of stocks to be analyzed. Your metrics will not cover stocks with special situations. For example, IBM always has had a high Price/Book value for as long as I can remember and therefore it does not mean it should be excluded.

The searches based on fundamental metrics help us to narrow stocks for further evaluation. Occasionally I abandon the scoring system for some stocks under special conditions.

Compare a company's metrics to its sector's averages
This could be the most powerful comparison: Compare Apples to Apples.

You may want to compare the metrics of a company to the averages of that sector. The average of supermarket's P/S is extremely low and hence it has no meaning to compare a supermarket's P/S to most other sectors. Some sectors like utilities need high debt to run a utility company.

However, when the average P/E or other metric of a sector is suddenly lower than its historical average, it could mean that sector is out-of-favor and/or the sector is having a better value.

This following table compares Apple to its sector and a retail sector on a specific date for illustration. All the metrics will change.

Metric	Apple	Computer	Retail
P/E	11	19	24
(5-year average)	16	17	15
PEG	.6	N/A	1.4
Price /Cash Flow	9.4	8.1	9.2
Price /Book	3.3	3.0	3.6
EPS Growth	-6%	-42%	2.6%
(last 5 years)	62%	45%	11%
Operating Margin	20%	15%	8%
ROE	30%	14%	19%
Debt / Equity	2%	7%	88%
Inventory Turnover	76%	53%	4.55x

From the above table, some metrics only make sense for an industrial sector (Computer for Apple). In this case, you may want to compare AAPL to Computer, and not to Retail.

"Debt / Equity" indicates that the retail sector needs to borrow more than the computer sector for example. Of course, retail stores have high Inventory Turnover.

Top-down approach

First, compare whether the market is risky. Second, select the best sector; there are many sites including Finviz.com to select the best sector. Then compare the fundamental metrics of the major stocks within that sector.

Some metrics do not apply

Using financial institutions as an example, usually P/B is more useful than P/CF. However, the quality of a loan (not a metric here) is more important than all metrics as we found out in 2007. P/S is more important for retails. However, the expected P/E is most important for most other sectors.

When you believe a sector is the currently best (a criterion available in many screeners), select the best stocks in this sector.

Compare metrics to its five-year average

If the company's five-year average of P/E (available from Fidelity and many other sites) is 20 and today it is 10. It is 100% under-valued by this standard. Also, you may want to try other metrics such as debt/equity and compare it to the five-year average.

Growth Metrics

The growth metrics are growth rates of the stock price, sales, earnings, etc. They are useful for growth investors.

Even for value investors, the earnings growth rate is very important, as most stocks with substantial gains have increased their earnings growth first. If the earnings has grown but the price remains the same (i.e., PEG), then the potential for price appreciation will be higher and most likely it will return to the historical average P/E.

Momentum Metrics

Momentum metrics is part of growth. The rates of increase of the stock price, the volume… are the major metrics. Earnings revision is another one especially in earnings announcement seasons (usually 4 times a year).

Fidelity and many subscription services provide a composite rank with name Timely or similar name. The following could be part of this Timely score: SMA-50, Q-Q sales increase and recent price appreciation. In my momentum portfolio, I use these metrics and ignore all the other metrics as my average holding period is less than 30 days for momentum strategies.

Insiders' buying

Insiders sell their stocks for many reasons. When insiders buy a lot of their companies' stocks at market prices, take notice. Insiders know better than anyone about the health of their companies and their industries.

Select Insiders' purchases from one of the available sites such as Finviz.com. Ignore the option exercises. I prefer the high ratios of Net Total Purchase Value / Market Cap and the purchases by more than one insider. Be careful that the insiders purchase the stocks after selling a similar amount of stock in a brief time span.

OpenInsider is a good site for this info.
InsiderSights is a good one too with more capable tools that would take more time to learn.

Where to get the metrics
You can get this information from the website with no or low cost such as Finviz.com, your broker's site, AAII (very low cost) and Fidelity.

The following subscriptions are at a little higher cost but they are still less than $1,000 per year: Value Line, IBD, Zacks, VectorVest and Stock Screen 123. Many data from different vendors are duplicated such as P/E. You will save time by concentrating on one or two sources.

Many vendors provide a composite metric such as a value metric to cover P/E, debt... and a timing metric to cover Technical Analysis indicators, PEG, price appreciation rate...

Short % is a useful metric available in Finviz.com. For Fidelity customers, you can click on Research and then Stock. Enter the stock name, and then click on Detailed. I find Fidelity's Analysts' Opinions quite useful.

Finviz.com provides a lot of useful information free of charge. It also provides a screen function. The 'Help' button describes Finviz's functions and all the metrics monitored.

Other sources are: Insider Cow, NASDAQ Guru Analysis ...

Monitor the recent performance of the metrics
The predictability of most metrics has proven not to perform consistently as many investors and fund managers found out. My theory is that the

specific metric works better in some market conditions than others. To test which ones work better currently, check their performance in the last three months and use those that perform well. This is what my scoring system in the book Scoring Stocks is based on.

Why some metrics fail sometimes
Most investors are using metrics to screen stocks, but few are successful consistently. Some investment companies have top analysts dedicated to projects looking for the right strategy. My guesses why they fail are:

1. Metrics need to be monitored to see its effectiveness on current market conditions.

2. Besides fundamental metrics, there are many intangibles.

3. When they have too many followers on the same metrics, they will not work such as ROE in the last several years.

4. Fundamentals need time (at least 6 months) to reflect the value of the stock. You're swimming against the tide as a fundamentalist. Trading momentum stocks using basic fundamentals will not work.

5. Watch out 'Garbage in and garbage out'. Some emerging countries do not have an organization similar to SEC to ensure the integrity of the financial statements of a company and some audit firms are being paid to cover their eyes. Even though there are frauds in some U.S. companies and with their auditors.

6. The metrics may be derived from obsolete financial statements. Check out the date. The most updated one could be available from the company's website.

7. Some companies borrow a lot of money to dress up the metrics such as P/E and ROE. They will look good short-term but not long-term. Ensure the debt/equity has not been increased recently for this purpose. I recall one utility spin-off had incredible fundamentals except the debt load. It is so high that all these fundamentals will deteriorate in the future due to servicing its high debts.

Footnote

[1] The stocks are classified into sector and then sectors are divided into industries (same as sub sectors). For example, oil is a sector and oil exploration and oil services are industries under the oil sector. For simplicity, I intermix the terms here as many sectors do not need further sub classifications for this discussion.

[2] AMZN is not a value stock by any standard. As of 1/1/2013, its P/E (from last 12 months) is 157 and P/B is 15. Both fall far into my low-range values. Its price rises from 256 from 1/1/13 to 270 today (1/22/13). Today its P/E is ridiculously over 3,000. The investors are betting AMZN's internet sales will take over the concrete stores and its investors do not care about profit but rather for market share. Does it sound familiar in the internet era? Its price momentum is indicated positively by any chart. It may be a good stock for traders, but it is too risky for a swing trader and a long-term investor like me (yes, I wear two hats). I do not short stocks in a rising market, but this could be an exception.

Afterthoughts

- The only recommendation from a very popular investment book I read is to select stocks by the return of equity (ROE). I will save you the time and money to read that book. I read the entire book in an hour at Barnes and Noble's and it saved me some money / time, not to mention cutting down trees for that book. Basically, it does not work today.
- DAL has an interesting Debt / Equity of over -1000% due to the negative equity. For a comparison, you may want to use Debt / ABS(Equity).
- Once in a while, I found the financial data was not consistent from different sources. Try to check out any discrepancy in the dates of the financial data of your sources. The financial statements from the company websites usually have the most updated data.
- Current Ratio = Current Asset / Current Liability. If it is below 1, then the company is having a tough time in meeting its current cash obligations.
- Dividend Yield is a valid metric for matured companies. I do not use it to evaluate growth companies or companies that need to plow back cash for research and development.

- If you use Finviz.com, you find three margins: profit, gross and operating. I prefer to use profit margin that is more useful for most companies. The other two may be relevant in some sectors.

    http://www.investopedia.com/terms/p/profitmargin.asp
    http://www.investopedia.com/terms/g/grossmargin.asp
    http://www.investopedia.com/terms/o/operatingmargin.asp

    Use Wikipedia for more description.
- Enron had millions in profits but negative cash flows. Earnings can be manipulated but not the cash flows.

    Insiders' selling usually does not cause any alarm unless excessively. Most insiders sell most of the stocks they have before these companies go bankrupt. Just common sense!
- Why fundamentals are important.
    (http://seekingalpha.com/article/1612442-its-shorting-season)

    On the same day when this article was published, RVLT was up 10% due to increasing sales in the earnings conference. However, the company is still not profitable. It shows how tough shorting is even with good arguments. That's why do not expect every purchase is profitable. However, with the educated guesses, you should beat the market in the long run.
- Due to my ignorance, limited time or my short period of holding stocks, I have not used intrinsic value that often.

    Book value is different from intrinsic value. Book value is calculated by summing up the values of all pieces of a company such as a building and all equipment. Intrinsic value is the real value of a company. When two companies have the same book value and market cap, the company that generates more profit than the other one usually has a higher intrinsic value. When the intrinsic value is higher than the stock price, it is underpriced in theory.

    Links:
    Income statement: https://www.youtube.com/watch?v=ht-tzwyLPU
    The following link provides more info on intrinsic value.
    http://en.wikipedia.org/wiki/Intrinsic_value_%28finance%29
    https://www.youtube.com/watch?v=l-T-Vyk2txc&authuser=0

Mysteries of P/E

If you believe you can make good money by selecting stocks with low P/Es solely, dream on. If it were that easy, there would be no poor folks. However, buying fundamentally sound companies would reduce the risk and improve the chance of its appreciation.

P/E is the most misunderstood indicator. To me, it is the most useful one among all metrics if it is properly used. Earnings are the key to stock appreciation and P/E measures its value. To illustrate on P/E, you pay a million for a hot-dog cart in NYC. Even if its earnings increase year after year, you will never recoup your investment as you have paid too much even for a good business.

"Buy stocks with P/E below 15 and earnings positive" is not true in many cases. P/E growth (PEG) should be considered at least as a prospect of the company. Many retailers were destroyed by Amazon and many newspapers were destroyed by Facebook and Google. Which sector do you want to buy: the sector in up trending or the dying sector even with a better P/E?

Most old books on value are based on old industries that are no longer applicable in today's market. Read these books but ask the above question.

Better definition
P/E should be inverted as E/P, which is termed as Earnings Yield. Earnings Yield is easy to be compared and understood. It takes care of negative earnings for screening stocks and ranking (comparing stocks with the better P/E first). If you sort P/E in ascending order, your order will be wrong with the negative earnings but right with E/P.

It is usually compared to a 10-year Treasury bill yield (or 30 years) or a CD rate. If the stock has 5% earnings yield and your one-year CD is 1%, then it beats the CD by 4% in absolute numbers and four times better. However, the CD is virtually risk free (with deposit amount limits in most banks). Earning yield is an estimated guess and it may not materialize.

Many ways to predict E/P
- Based on the last 12 months. Project it to the Forward E/P. It is also called the last twelve-month E/P.

- Based on analysts' educated guesses. Guesses may not materialize. Based on my experience, the expected usually predicts better than the one based on the last 12 months. This is the one I use most and many investing subscriptions provide this Forward P/E (same as the Expected P/E) or expected E/P.

Usually, I do not trust the analyst's opinions due to their conflict of interest. However, the earnings estimate is my exception.

- Based on the last month or the last quarter. Latest information could be better for predictions. However, they are not good for seasonal businesses such as the retail where most sales are done during the Christmas season.
- Besides the Pow PE described later; I take the average of the earnings yield EY as:

The Avg. EY = (EY from the last twelve month + Expected EY + EY from the current month of prior year) / 3

It averages out using figures from the past, the present and the future. If no one has used it, I claim shamelessly it is my original idea.

Best E/P could not be the best
Very high E/P could be signs of troubles ahead such as a lawsuit pending, fraud, etc. If you find companies E/P over 50%, it means two years' profits could be equal to the entire cost of the company! I can tell you right away that they probably smell fishy unless you believe that there is a free lunch in life.

However, from time to time, some bargains do exist due to certain conditions, or the Wall Street is just wrong about the company. I found one in my year-end screen and that gave me huge return. You need to find out whether they are bargains or traps. When the E/P is low (sometimes even negative) but is improving fast, it could mean big profits for you. Fundamentalists may miss this opportunity in the early stages due to the unfavorable E/P, but it could be the most profitable time to buy. Sometimes, it could be a turnaround.

During a recession, most good companies have a hard time in promoting new products as the consumers are thrifty. At the same time, it usually is the best time to develop products if they have enough cash to finance them. In this case, there will be no alarm even with negative earnings. The only alarm is when a company cannot meet the debt obligations.

Some companies can manipulate earnings via dirty tricks in accounting. It could make this year look really good, but it is harder or even impossible to continue the same trick for many years. Check out the footnotes in the financial statement.

E/P and PEG

For value investing, E/P is usually used and the higher the better. Watch out when it is extraordinarily high.

PEG (P/E growth) measures the rate of improving P/E. '1' is supposed to be neutral to most investors. When it is below 1, it is undervalued, and vice versa.

PEG = (P/E) / Earnings Growth Rate

They have a similar problem with P/E with negative earnings.

Which of the following two stocks do you want to buy based on their historical earning yields and earnings growth?

1. A stock that has a 10% earnings yield with no earnings growth.
2. A stock that has an 8% earnings yield with 50% earnings growth.

If the earnings growth continues, in next year the second stock should pay 12%, substantially better than the first stock. This is another reason we should use forward earnings rather than historical earnings.

PEG may give a low value for companies that pay high dividends. To correct it,

PEG = (P/E)/ (Earning Growth Rate + Dividend Yield)

When the general market favors growth stocks, weigh more on growth metrics including PEG. I claim no credit on the adjusted PEG.

Fundamental metrics

E/P is one of the metrics you should use but not exclusively. If the earning yield is high but the % of debt is high too, then a good bargain may not be as good as it appears to be.

Some other metrics may not be easily found in the financial statements such as the intangibles, insider buying, pension obligations, trade secrets, losing market share, brand name, customers' loyalty, etc. It is interesting that most metrics change its ability to predict from time to time.

P/E variations

There are other P/E variations like Shiller P/E (same as CAPE and PE10). Shiller P/E can also be used to track the current market valuation. It is controversial and its value is easily misinterpreted. Hence, use it as a reference only unless you understand all its issues. I prefer to use a two-year average of the P/E instead of 10 as I believe the market changes too much over a ten-year span. Currently Shill P/E does not work that well as before. It is due to the excessive printing of money.

Compare a company's current P/E to its average P/E in the last 5 years. Also compare it to the average value of the companies in the same industry. The average P/E for high-tech companies is different from supermarkets for example. They are available from Fidelity.

P/E is more reliable for a group of stocks (SPY for example) instead of individual stocks which have too many other metrics and intangibles to deal with. When you compare the total return of an ETF to a corresponding index, you need to add the respective dividends to the index to ensure a fair comparison of total returns. As of this writing, the S&P 500 is paying about a 2% dividend.

EV/EBITDA is another way to measure the value of a company. This metric has its advantages and disadvantages over P/E. It includes other important data such as cash and debt. EBITDA/EV is equivalent to E/P including other mentioned metrics. I prefer to use it over E/P. Some sites do not provide it if the earnings is negative. The disadvantage to me is it does not use expected earnings. This ratio can be found under Yahoo!Finance.

Garbage in, garbage out
I do not trust most financial statements from emerging countries, especially the smaller companies. Watch out for fraudulent data. Most metrics can be manipulated. Recently I have a US stock that lost 18% in one day due to the SEC's investigation of its financial data.

The announced earnings may not be reflected in the financial statements that you use from the web. Ensure your data is up-to-date by checking the date of the financial statements. Seeking Alpha has transcripts for the earnings announcements that would save you a trip to attend the companies' quarterly meetings.

Sector and entire market

You can find the value of a sector using the P/E of an ETF for that sector. It is similar for the market. For example, use SPY (an ETF simulating the S&P 500 index). If it is lower than the average (15 to me), then most likely the market is good value and a buy signal. It is one of the many hints for market timing.

Where to use P/E

Each highlight of the following corresponds to one of my books. Click it for the description of the strategy.

My book on top-down approach starts with a safe market, then sector analysis, fundamental analysis, intangible analysis and optionally technical analysis. P/E is one of the many metrics in fundamental analysis.

There are many styles of investing. In general, fundamental analysis is important when you hold the stock longer.

- P/E is important in Long-Term Swing, Dividend Investing, Retirees and Conservative Strategies.
- My max value is 20 and 25 for tech companies. I ignore it if they have high potential for appreciation that could be indicated by insider purchases. However, many unknown companies then had a P/E over 50. Tesla had a P/E over 1,000 at one time.
- P/E is moderately important in Short-Term Swing and Sector Rotation.
- P/E is the least important in Momentum Strategy and Day Trading.

Summary

Again, one metric should not dictate the reason to trade a stock. Compare the company P/E to its industry average and its own five-year average. In addition, many industries have cycles. If you buy it at the peak of the industry, the P/E may mislead you. Besides fundamental analysis, you need to consider intangible analysis and time the entry / exit point by using technical analysis. Intangible analysis evaluates information that cannot be summarized into numeric metrics such as a lawsuit pending.

True P/E

"EV/EBITDA" is available from Yahoo!Finance and other sources. The true EY is "1/Ture PE". I call it "True" for the lack of a better term as it represents the financial situation of the company better. This could be the most important metric for many.

EBITDA: https://www.youtube.com/watch?v=C2eoh3X4efM

Earnings can be manipulated. For example, the company management can lower the P/E ratio by buying back its stocks. In this case the earnings per share is boosted but in reality, there is no change in the company's financial fundamentals. The true P/E takes into consideration the reduced cash. EBITBA stands for "Earnings Before Interest, Taxes, Depreciation, and Amortization".

Be careful when EV or "EBITDA" is negative. Most likely you should avoid the stocks with a negative EV.

Yahoo!Finance usually leaves EV/EVITDA blank for financial institutions such banks, loan companies and REITS. In this case, use forward earnings yield (= 1 / Forward P/E or Pow Earnings Yield described next.

I prefer True Yield based on Forward P/E instead of P/E as it has better predictable power to me. To illustrate, Apple has a P/E of 21.61, Forward P/E of 19.46 (both from Finviz), and Enterprise Value / EBIT of 16.72 (from Yahoo!Finance). The True Yield is 6% (1/16.72). The True Yield based on Forward P/E is 7% (6% * 21.61/19.48).

Pow P/E
You should use the described "EV/EBITDA" and hence "Pow P/E" can be ignored. There are some cases that Pow P/E is better: 1. "EV/EBITDA" may not be available for reasons such as negative asset and 2. Use of Forward Earnings instead of Earnings based on the last twelve months. The following is an exercise on how I simulate it from Finviz.com with metrics that are readily available.

I modified P/E to take care of cash and debts. I use my last name due to being easier to distinguish from P/E and it has nothing to do with my ego.

Pow P/E = (P - Cash per Share + Debt per Share) / (Earning - Interest gained per share - Interest paid per share)

Pow Earnings Yield = 1 / Pow P/E

Here is a comparison of E/P (Earnings Yield), Expected Earnings Yield (Forward E/P), True Yield (EBITD/EV) and Pow Earning Yields, which is based one Forward (Expected) Earnings as of 10/14/2021.

	CARS	MPAA
Earnings Yield	1%	7%
Expected Earnings Yield	12%	12%
True Yield	13%	11%
Pow Earnings Yield	5%	9%

P/E is not always important

The following is my test from 1/2/2020 to 10/14/2020. RSP is similar to SPY except that the stocks in the S&P 500 index are equally weighted. EY (= E/P) is Expected Earnings Yield and there are no stocks with EY less than 0. DY is Dividend Yield. GPE is the growth of P/E. As in my book, I use annualized returns and dividends are not included. This test does not mean a lot, but it tells us what these metrics behave during this period, or it indicates **Value is not a good metric in this period**, and it may indicate momentum is better in this period. Most big winners start as small companies with **high P/E** (from 30 to 100). Many of them have important technologies or special systems that would change the world such as Microsoft, Facebook, Amazon and Walmart to name a few. Their sales have increased substantially year after year.

Examples of not depending on low P/Es. Before the financial crisis in 2008, P/Es of most bank stocks had 10-year low. After they announced the earnings, P/Es of many of them surged to over 100 and the stock prices suffered losses of more than 80% within 12 months. The stock price of Bethlehem Steel with P/E of 2 at one time went to zero. Need to find out why the stock is so cheap via intangible analysis and qualitative analysis.

The following is very rough testing and there are many limitations in the database. However, the conclusion is quite convincing to me and some are opposite to the contrary beliefs. For example, I expected the higher EY the better, but not in this test.

	Ann. Return	Indicator	Comment
RSP 500 All	-2%		
EY (top 10)	-54%	Bad	Contrary
GPE (top 10)	-20%	Bad	Contrary

Select All or top 100.			
DY = 0	16%	Good	
DY (top 100)	-19%	Bad	
DY / 1 and 2	2%		
EY 3 to 4	15%	Good	Second best
EY 2 to 3	6%	Good	Third best
EY 1 to 2	31%	Good	Best
EY 0 to 1	-39%	Bad`	

I use some metrics from a service I subscribe to that are not included here. Two major metrics of this subscription have a return of around 20%. Most subscriptions including the free Fidelity (to some extent) give you three composite scores: Total, Fundamental and Timing. I wish to check out the recent predictability of Fidelity's Equity Summary Score if they have a historical database. Most of them take out the delisted and /or bankrupt companies in their databases.

Link: P/E: https://www.youtube.com/watch?v=4KkTGx2bK_4

Testing key metrics

Here is a summary table on my findings in a recent test. It is based on a small amount data from 1-5-2007 to 1-7-2014 (about one market cycle). This is for illustrating how to test metrics and I am not responsible for any error in preparing the results.

Metric	P/E	PEG	P/S	P/FC	P/B
Criteria	<3	<1	<.06	<10	<2

I used P/E growth rate of P/E instead of PEG and it is 8%. My average P/S is about .07, substantially smaller than .8 from other tests. If you have a historical database, you can test it out the above metrics and other metrics with the criteria described below.

Common testing criteria
The following are my basic criteria.
- Market Cap > 50 M.
- Price > 1 to reduce survivorship bias.
- Avg. Volume > 10,000.
- 3 Major Exchanges.
- EPS > 0. Only select stocks with positive earnings.

I started from 2007 and ended in 2013. I tested from the beginning of the year (actually with several days later due to no data on Jan. 1) to the end of the year. Repeat it for the next year and average the returns of all the 7 years. I call it 'window' testing to avoid the distorted value when you have a big win or loss in the early year.

To illustrate, I tested the above criteria with P/E and sort P/E in ascending order from 1/5/2007 to 1/4/2008. The top 10 stocks have an average of 44%. Repeated the test for the next 7 years.

Result
Here is the partial result

Metric	P/E	PEG	P/S	SPY
Avg. Return	13%	8%	38%	6%
Beat SPY	124%	35%	538%	N/A

However, from my Market Timing book, I should be out of the stock market in second part of 2007 and the entire 2008. The next table is from 2009 to 2013 instead of from 2007 and resembles my actual trading better.

Metric	P/E	PEG	P/S	SPY
Avg. Return	35%	19%	125%	13%
Beat SPY	166%	45%	864%	N/A

The above metrics beat SPY by a larger percent in the 'good' years than the first table.

P/B and P/FC (Free Cash) are obtained info from other sources. I also had P/S Growth and it did not beat SPY. It is ignored. P/S turns out to be very important metric.

To illustrate such as the 3 in P/E, I selected the highest value of the P/E in the top 10 stocks for each year and averaged the values from 5 tests (from 2009).

Instead of holding the stocks for 1 year, I tried 2 years. The result is worse, so stick with holding the stocks for 1 year.

The next step is to find the best combination in more than one metric and their values, such as "P/S < .06" and "P/E < 3". If I do not find a lot of stocks, I would relax the criteria such as "P/S < .08 and "P/E < 4".

This is just a general guideline. Different sectors have different metrics. Super market has a very different P/S than high tech companies for example.

Technical indicators

Bring up Finviz.com from your browser and enter the symbol of the stock.

Ensure the stock's SMA200 is above 0% as we do not want to buy stock in a downward trend. SMA200% is Single Moving Average for the last 200 trade sessions. The percent indicates how far the stock price from its SMA.

In addition, the RSI(14) should be less than 75, which would indicate the stock is overbought.

My calculation on SPY compared to MSN is a little off for the following reasons: 1. Not starting on Jan. 1 and ending on Dec. 31 for my convenience, and 2. Dividends are not included. As long as I use the same dates for other tests, it is quite OK for comparing with my test results. For better total return estimate, add 2% for dividend to my SPY for the annualized rate and then the difference is about 1%.

	My SPY (Few days diff)	MSN (with dividend)	Difference
Avg. 3 years	13%	17%	3%
Avg. 5 years	6%	9%	3%

Summary table

Metric	Value	Indicates	Relaxed
Market: (use SPY)			
SMA350%	Above 0	Not plunging	Above 0

SMA350%	>9	Correction possible	>12
RSI(14)	>65	Correction possible	>70
Fundamentals:			
P/E	<4	Good	<8
PEG	<1	Good	<1.2
P/S	<.07 (or even # .8)	Good	<.8
Technical:			
SMA200%	>0	Up trend	>1
SMA200%	<10	Not peaking	<15
RSI(14)	<70	Not overbought	<75

Relaxed values are what I use.

2   Finviz's parameters

Most metrics are described in Finviz (via Help), Investopedia and/or Wikipedia and my articles on P/E and fundamental metrics if available. We use the metrics for screening stocks and then evaluating the screened stocks.

The following are my personal comments and why I feel some metrics are more important than the others. Personally, I divide the metrics into fundamentals and technical, which are more important for long-term investors and short-term investors respectively.

Compare the ratios to the companies in the same sector (industry) and also its averages from the last few years (5 preferable) from many other websites such as Fidelity.

From your browser, enter Finviz.com. Enter a symbol (I used ABEO for discussion). A chart is displayed with the prices and volumes for the last eleven months. SMAs (Single Moving Average) are displayed sometimes with other technical indicators. Intraday, Daily and Weekly options are available for day traders, short-term traders and long-term traders respectively. I prefer Candle – Advanced for drawing charts.

Besides the chart and the metrics described next, it describes what the company does, analysts' recommendations (I prefer Fidelity's Equity Summary Score), insiders' trading and articles that are good for intangible and qualitative analysis. Many free websites such as Yahoo!Finance provide a list of articles about the company.

"Financial Highlights and Statements" are materials for more in-depth analysis and they were more important decades ago when most financial ratios had not been calculated for you. It is important for investors with good knowledge in financial accounting. The current version also includes the basic balance sheet, income statement and cash flow for the current (TTM) and the last two years. Click on the following YouTube links for more detail.

Balance: https://www.youtube.com/watch?v=DMv9JC_K37Y
Income: https://www.youtube.com/watch?v=O--AvwZabIQ
Cash flow: https://www.youtube.com/watch?v=hMBN6yTIDb0

A section on Insider Trading is also included. Do not be alarmed when insiders dump small quantities of the stocks. Buying large quantities (e.g., insider transaction more than 5%) at prices close to the market price could be favorable news.

The following metrics are roughly based on the flow of Finviz from top to bottom and left to right. I skip those metrics that I believe are not too important. You can also place your cursor on the metric to retrieve the description from Finviz or via Finviz's Help. Some metrics are left blank to indicate they are not applicable (for example, zero, negative or not available). For example, the Debt/Equity of YRCW in 1/2019 is blank (same as null) due to its negative Equity. From Yahoo!Finance at the time of writing, it has a total debt of 888M.

- **Index**. Most of us trade stocks in the three major exchanges in the USA. Stocks listed over-the-counter are too risky for most of us. Skip the stocks in local exchanges and foreign exchanges unless you are an expert on these stocks and/or have insightful (not illegal info from insiders) information. I screen the stocks and then ignore the stocks that are not in the Dow, NASDAQ and Amex. Other screeners may let you select a group of exchanges.

- **Market Cap** (MC). To me, stocks below 50M are risky even though they could be very profitable. Ensure the Avg. Volume is at least 10,000 shares and / or your order is less than 1% of the average volume. Some small stocks are controlled by the owners and have small volumes. You cannot trade these stocks easily.

Float = Outstanding shares – Insider shares

Usually, Float does not matter as they are typically the same. However, it does for small companies with large insider shares. Most of these owners do not want to sell their family businesses and hence they reduce the chance of being acquired entirely or partially for good prices. In this case, you may have to hold this kind of stock for a long time or you may have to sell it at a very unfavorable price.

- If **Forward P/E** (a.k.a. Expected P/E) is not provided, use the P/E which is based on the trailing last 12 months (TTM). Alternatively, calculate the E by using the E from P/E and multiplying it by its growth rate. It may not be seasonally adjusted. I prefer using Forward P/E as it provides a better predictability power to me. Successful investing is usually a result of correct guessing the future earnings.

Finviz.com leaves the P/E blank (same as null) if the earnings are negative. In this case, I would check out Yahoo!Finance's EV / EBITDA, which also considers taxes, cash and interests. The blank condition also happens in some other metrics such as negative assets (very seldom).

Earnings Yield is equal to E/P. I call it 'True Earnings Yield' for EBITDA / EV. It is easier to understand. Compare Earnings Yield or True Yield to the annual dividend yield of a 10-year Treasury – with the low interest rate in 2021, skip this comparison for this year.

E/P is easier in screening and sorting the screened stocks. If you use P/E instead of E/P, you need to screen or sort stocks with a clause "P/E > 0".

When the P/E is less than 5, be careful and there may be a reason why it is so low. Many bankrupting companies have low P/Es at one time before their stock prices go to zero..

Compare the P/E or Forward P/E with the average P/E for the sector (such as high tech) and its average P/E for the last 5 years that are currently available from Fidelity.com. Some sectors such as technology have high P/Es (such as 25 for me). If the sector is cyclical, the earnings could be affected.

Do not solely use P/E to determine the value of a stock. The other metrics are P/E Growth (PEG), P/B, Debt/Equity to name a few.

When the prospect of the company is good such as Tesla in 2020, ignore P/E. Investors are betting on the future. Do not short these rocket stocks.

- **Cash / share**. It is used to calculate Pow P/E and Pow EY when EV/EBITDA for the stock is not available. To illustrate, if the stock is $10 and it has $10 cash / share without debt (i.e., Debt/Equity = 0), most likely it is underpriced as you can get the whole company for nothing. You should find out why the price is so low. It could be the market ignoring the stock, or there is a serious event happening such as a major lawsuit. P/C is a better choice than Cash/Share; the lower the better.
- **Dividend %** is useful for income investors. The payout ratio should not be more than 30% except for matured companies. Most developing companies and tech companies plough back the profits into research and development, and hence they do not pay dividends.
- **Recs**. Select stocks with 1 or 2. Do not base your stock selection on this recommendation alone. There have been many bad recommendations that could cost you a fortune in losses. Use Fidelity's Equity Summary Score instead.
- **PEG** is a measure of the growth of P/E and hence a growth metric (the other ones are Sales Growth Q-Q and Earnings Growth Q-Q). It is similar to P/E, but it takes the expected earnings growth rate into account. The lower value is better as long as earnings is positive. If earnings is negative, then the reverse is true. It is a defect in using P/E and PEG and that's why I recommend EY (Earnings Yield) and EYG, Earnings Yield Growth. The chance of appreciation of the stock is high when the PEG is less than 1.

If there are two companies with the same P/E, the one with a better PEG ratio is better. For similar logic, if two companies have the same E/P, the company with higher Earnings Growth (EPS Q/Q) would be better.

- **P/B**. Book value or Asset (= Total Assets – Total Liabilities) may not include intangible assets such as patents. Do not trust it 100%, so is ROE and other metrics which are based on the book value. Negative equity is possible when Total Liabilities is more than Total Assets. This popular metric is outdated for most matured companies as it is now made up of more intangible assets including patents, management, the quality of their employees, brand names, market share, partners, free cash flow and customer base to name a few. Some assets such as gold mines and real estates can be easily calculated. To illustrate, when gold price is falling, the P/B of a company's stock could be less than 1. It could be a good buy, but it is not if the trend continues downward.
- **P/S**. If two companies are unprofitable, this ratio could be more useful. A retail company such as Walmart is very different from a research company in P/S. This metric is only meaningful for stocks within the same sector or related sectors.
- **P/FCF**. I prefer it to be greater than 0 and less than 50 for value investors. Most metrics can be manipulated easily, but not this one. This is a major metric to avoid bankrupting companies.
- **Sales Q/Q** reduces the seasonal deviation. To illustrate, retail sales for the Christmas season should be compared to the same season in the prior year.
- **EPS Q/Q**. Same as above. I prefer the growth of EPS over Sales. Both of these Q/Q ratios are growth metrics. When a company terminates its unprofitable product(s), its Sales Q/Q could be down but its EPS Q/Q could be up. In 2000, many internet companies had great Sales Q/Qs but negative EPS Q/Qs.

Q/Q comparison (quarter to quarter) takes out the seasonal variations as Sales Q/Q. I prefer both Sales Q/Q and EPS Q/Q increase. When EPS Q/Q increases far higher than Sales Q/Q, it could mean the EPS Q/Q could be temporary such as the oil company when the oil price rockets. When the company buys its own shares, EPS could be misleading as E is fixed and the number of shares is reduced. In most cases, the fundamentals of the company have not changed.

In 2021, many companies such as many energy stocks have incredible EPS Q-Q and most of their Forward P/E are better than the P/E. They could be momentum play unless they are sustainable.

- Positive **Insider** Transactions are favorable. Sometimes, they are misleading. Need to scroll to the end of the screen and check out more info there. If the transactions are outdated such as 3 months or so ago, and or they are purchases in a similar amount than the sales a while ago, they are not important. Insiders know the company better than us.

So is **Institutional Transactions** as institutional investors move the market. Most institutional investors do not trade small stocks, and hence this metric is not important for small cap stocks.

- Insider Own, Shares Outstanding and Shares **Float** determine the number of shares that are available for trading. The stock with a small Float and a high Insider Own limits trading and the stock, and hence it should be avoided in most cases. Also, compare your trade positions for this kind of stock to their Avg. Volumes.
- **Profit Margin**. I prefer it over Gross Margin and Oper. Margin which does not include interest expenses and taxes. When you sell software, the Gross Margin is high as it does not include development, support and marketing, etc. A retail store has low Gross Margin. It all depends on the industry, and hence it is better to compare companies in the same industry.
- **Short Float**. I prefer it to be less than 10%. If it is greater than 10%, the shorters could find something wrong with the company. If it is over 25%, I would check the fundamentals and any important events such as a major lawsuit. If they are good, I would buy it expecting a short squeeze potential. It is risky but it has been proven profitable in some of my trades.
- Technical metrics: SMA-20, SMA-50 and SMA-200. Finviz expresses them in convenient percentages. If they are all positive, it means the trend is up. SMA-20 and SMA-50 are a short-term trend indicator and SMA-200 is a long-term trend indicator. If you are a short-term swing investor, stick with the short-term trend and vice versa. The first two are also used as momentum grades. Many long-term investors do not buy stocks when the SMA-200% is negative. Some buy stocks when both SMA-20 and SMA-50 are positive and SMA-20 crosses SMA-50,. Some sell the owned stocks when both SMA-20 and SMA-50 are negative and SMA-20 crosses SMA-50. Some use SMA-50 and SMA-200 instead. They are called the Golden Cross and the Death Cross.
- **RSI(14)**. If it is greater than 65%, it is overbought to me. If it is under 30%, it is under-bought for me to me. Some use 5% up or down than my percentages. Use it as a reference. Most stocks making new heights are always overbought, and many of these stocks keep on rising. I recommend using trailing stops to protect your profits on rising stocks.
- **Beta**. A volatile stock fluctuates a lot. Higher beta stocks are good for short-term traders. A beta of 1 means the stock would fluctuate with

the market, and it is more volatile if it is higher than 1. For volatile stocks (higher than 1), the stops should be higher. For example, if your stops are normally 10%, you may want to use 15% or even higher for volatile stocks.
- **Perf**. If the stock lost more than 50%, there is a good chance it could be a candidate for bottom fishing, or it could be heading to bankruptcy. Need more research if you want to buy these risky stocks.
- Management performance is measured by **ROE**. It is also judged by **Analysts' Rec.** and Institutional Ownership (except for small companies). The confidence of their own ability, the company and its sector are measured by Insider Ownership and Insider Purchases.
ROE = Net Income / Average Shareholder's Equity

According to Investopedia, a normal ROE for utilities should be 10% while high tech companies should be 15%. Compare this ratio and many other ratios with its peers that are available from many sites including Fidelity.
- Avoid all companies that are going to bankrupt at all costs. Debt/Equity, P/FCF, Cash/Sh., P/B, Profit Margin, Forward P/E, Short Float, RSI(14), SMA20% and SMA50 would give us some hints. Need to summarize all the info and study many other factors such as obsoleting products (including drugs going to be generic). Study articles which are available from Finviz and many other sites.
- Unless you have concrete information, do not buy stocks a week or so before the Earnings Date (available in Finviz). It is seldom to make great profits when the announcement is better than the expected as the stock price is usually priced in, and the reverse could hurt the stock price a lot.

More useful information:
- **Equity** = Total Asset – Total Liability. When the Equity (Book) is negative, many of the metrics based on Equity would not be displayed. In May 5, 2022, TUP has Equity of -207M (from Finviz's Balance Sheet reported on 12/25/21). The related metrics are blank or null such as P/B, Debt/Eq, LT Debt/Eq in Finviz, and so is EV/EVITDA (from Yahoo!Finace). However, the P/E is less than 4. It could be a buy.
- The price chart. It has a lot of features such as the resistance line. Some charts include technical indicators such as double top (a bearish warning) and double bottom (a bullish sign).
- Description under the symbol. It briefly describes what the company (sector and industry) does and its country of registration. You want to

buy a stock within a sector that is trending up. For example, according to Finviz Apple is in the Consumer Goods sector and the Electronic Equipment industry.

If you do not want to buy foreign stocks, skip it if it is not listed in the US exchange or headquartered in a foreign country. Buying a foreign stock could be profitable, but risky due to the currency fluctuation, lack of regulations, and politics (such as Russia in 2022 and China in 2021). Some foreign stocks ask you to pay additional taxes when you sell them. Some foreign companies listed in the U.S. exchanges take out a good portion of the dividends.

- Articles on the company for qualitative analysis.
- Insider trading. Pay more attention to the insider purchases at market prices. Use common sense.
- The last line lets you open Yahoo!Finance and other sites.
- There are many ways to calculate intrinsic value of a stock. Many web sites (most require subscriptions) include this information. Use it as reference only, and evaluate the stock your yourself. Buy it when the intrinsic value is below the stock price, and sell it otherwise. It is "Buy Low and Sell High" concept. They work in general and in the long run. Need to consider other intangibles. Many stocks such as Tesla and Amazon had low intrinsic values, but they kept on rising.

Other important sites

Yahoo!Finance.

From Statistics, you can find Enterprise Value / EBITDA. I call it True Yield when I flip them to EBITDA / Enterprise Value. In case it is not available, I use Earnings Yield. In my spreadsheet without considering the cell designations,
=IF (Earnings Yield = "", True Yield, Earnings Yield)

Fidelity

Compare the P/E of the average PE of the last 5 years by using spreadsheets.
Cheaper By Historically =IF(PE="","",(Avg. of 5-year PE -PE)/Avg. of 5-year PE)

Compare the P/E of companies in the same sector. In my spreadsheet for demonstration,
Cheaper By To the peers =IF(PE="","",(Industry PE - PE)/Industry PE)

Your broker's website

Your broker website should have plenty of tools to analyze stocks. As of Dec., 2018, Fidelity lets you use their extensive research free by opening an account with no position restriction. I describe some of their metrics that should be beneficial to your research.

- Equity Summary Score. Potentially good buy when it is 7 (8 for conservative investors) or higher. With some exceptions, you should avoid buy or short stocks if the score is 3 or below. The stocks ranking from 4 to 6 could be turnaround candidates if they are supported by good Q/Q Earnings and/or good news. The above are my suggestions.

- The 5-year averages are good yardsticks. For example, in Dec., 2018, C's P/E is about 9 and the average for the last 5 years is 14. Hence it is a value buy.

Other sources

If you have other sources (most require a subscription or being a customer), skip the stocks that have one of the failing grades. The exceptions are a new positive development and increased insider purchases.

Vendor	Grade	Fail
Fidelity	Equity Summary Score	< 7
IBD	Composite grade	< 50
Value Line	Proj. 3-5 yr. return. Also, its composite rating	< 3%
Zacks	Rank	5
VectorVest	VST	< 0.7

You may be able to find Value Line and IBD in your local library. Try out the free stock reports from your broker first. Finviz and Seeking Alpha should have articles (now fewer free articles from Seeking Alpha) on stocks and earnings conferences, which could have important information after separating from the "welcome" and garbage talks.

Yahoo!Finance has good info. "EV/EBITDA" is better than "P/E" as it considers debts and cash. Most use Earnings from the last 12 months, which has poorer predictability than Forward Earnings to me.

When negative values such as Equity in Finviz.com, we need to adjust many related metrics or do not use them at all.

MarketWatch.com has many articles on the market in general and personal investing.

If the stock is close to the Earnings Date (found in Finviz.com), you should avoid trading the stock; as earnings could have a big swing for the stock price. Consult Zacks' ranking which is currently free for individual stocks.

Gurus

It is nice to know how gurus would rate the interested stocks. GuruFocus is a good source but requires subscription. NASDAQ is a simplified version. Bring up Nasdaq.com from your browser. Select "Investing" and then "Guru Screeners". On the third selection, enter the stock symbol such as THO. Click "Go". You will find how 10 or so gurus would evaluate this stock in theory. Click "Detailed Analysis" for each guru.

Quick and dirty

Many times we need to evaluate a stock fast such as taking action due to some development. Or, when you have over 30 stocks from your screen, you may want to reduce the number by using the following two methods.

Refer to my other article "Simplest way to evaluate stocks". The following should take a few minutes. Bring up Finviz.com and enter the stock symbol.

Using SWKS on 6/10/16 to illustrate, Forward P/E is about 11 (fine between 3 and 25), Debt/Eq. is 0 (fine less than .5), ROE is 30% (fine greater than 5%) and P/PCF is 31 (fine if not negative).

Also, check out Market Cap, Avg. Volume, Dividend, Short Float (fine between 0% and 10%), Country and Industry. Judging from the above, it is a buy.

If you have more time, check out the following: Recom. (Ok if less than 2.5), P/B (fine between .5 and 4), Sales Q/Q (fine if not negative), EPS Q/Q (fine if not negative), Cash/Sh (compare it to Debt/Sh) and Profit Margin (fine >5%). Check some articles described for this stock.

5-minute stock evaluation

It takes even less time than the above "Quick and Dirty". However, I recommend you should spend more time researching stocks.

- From Finviz.com, enter the stock or ETF symbol. Look at the number of reds in metrics. If there are more than greens, most likely it is not a good stock.

- It should be fine if Fidelity's Equity Summary Score is greater than 8.

If you have more time, I recommend you to check the following:

- Check out Forward P/E (E>0 and P/E < 20), Debut / Equity (< 50%) and P/FCF (not in red color).

  If time is allowed, replace Forward P/E with True P/E (same as "EV/EBITDA"), which is available from Yahoo!Finance and other sources.
- SMA20 (or SMA50 for longer holding period). If SMA20 is > 10%, it is trending up.

- It is fine if the Insider Transaction is positive.
- Be cautious on foreign stocks and low-volume stocks.
- If most of the above are positive, it is likely a buy. As in life, nothing is 100% certain.

Links

PEG: http://en.wikipedia.org/wiki/PEG_ratio
Short %: http://www.investopedia.com/university/shortselling/shortselling1.asp#axzz2LNDvpemo
Openinsider: http://www.openinsider.com/
Finviz: http://Finviz.com/
terms: http://www.Finviz.com/help/screener.ashx
Insider Cow: http://www.insidercow.com/
Current Ratio: http://en.wikipedia.org/wiki/Current_ratio
Cash Flow: https://www.youtube.com/watch?v=1v8hRZ36--c
How to find quality stocks.
http://seekingalpha.com/article/2381395-how-to-identify-quality-stocks-and-is-there-really-alpha-to-be-had
Over-priced stock: https://www.youtube.com/watch?v=VeMr0n4pvtM:
Outperform the market
https://www.youtube.com/watch?v=3DdY0JdUilM
Balance sheet: https://www.youtube.com/watch?v=DZjU0CHKyV4
Reading financial sheet.
https://www.youtube.com/watch?v=DMv9JC_K37Y&t=954s
https://www.youtube.com/watch?v=8NelYFn07jg
Intrinsic Value: https://www.youtube.com/watch?v=l-T-Vyk2txc

2   Finviz's parameters

Most metrics are described in Finviz (via Help), Investopedia and/or Wikipedia and my chapters on P/E and fundamental metrics if available. We use the metrics for screening stocks and then evaluating the screened stocks.

The following are my personal comments and why I feel some metrics are more important than the others. Personally I divide the metrics into fundamentals and technical, which are more important for long-term investors and short-term investors respectively.

Compare the ratios to the companies in the same sector (industry) and also its averages from the last few years (5 preferable) from many other websites such as Fidelity.

From your browser, enter Finviz.com. Enter a symbol (I used ABEO for discussion). A chart is displayed with the prices and volumes for the last eleven months. SMAs (Single Moving Average) are displayed sometimes with other technical indicators. Intraday, Daily and Weekly options are available for day traders, short-term traders and long-term traders respectively.

Besides the chart and the metrics described next, it describes what the company does, analysts' recommendations (I prefer Fidelity's Equity Summary), insiders' trading and articles that are good for intangible and qualitative analysis. Many free websites such as Yahoo!Finance may provide a list of articles about the company.

"Financial Highlights and Statements" are materials for more in-depth analysis and they were more important decades ago when most financial ratios had not been calculated for you. It is important for investors with good knowledge in financial accounting. The current version also includes basic financial statements and cash flow for the current (TTM) and the last two years.

A section on Insider Trading is also included. Do not be alarmed when insiders dump small quantities of the stocks. Buying large quantities (e.g. insider transaction more than 5%) at prices close to the market price could be favorable news.

The following metrics are roughly based on the flow of Finviz from top to bottom and left to right. I skip those metrics that I believe are not too important. You can also place your cursor on the metric to retrieve the description from Finviz. Some metrics are left blank to indicate they are not applicable (zero, negative or not available). For example, the Debt/Equity of YRCW in 1/2019 is blank (same as null) due to its negative Equity. From Yahoo!Finance at the time of writing, it has a total debt of 888M.

- **Index**. Most of us trade stocks in the three major exchanges in the USA. Stocks listed over-the-counter are too risky for most of us. Skip the stocks in local exchanges and foreign exchanges unless you are an expert on these stocks and/or have insightful (not insider) information. I screen the stocks and then ignore the stocks that are not in the Dow, NASDAQ and Amex. Other screeners may let you select a group of exchanges.

- **Market Cap** (MC). To me, stocks below 50M are risky even though they could be very profitable. Ensure the Avg. Volume is at least 10,000 shares and / or your order is less than 1% of the average volume. Some small stocks are controlled by the owners and have small volumes. In this case you cannot sell your stock easily.

  Float = Outstanding shares – Insider shares.

  Usually Float does not matter as they are typically the same. However, it does for small companies with large insider shares. Most of these owners do not want to sell their family businesses and hence they reduce the chance of being acquired entirely or partially for good prices. In this case, you may have to hold this stock for a long time or you sell it at a very unfavorable price.

- If **Forward P/E** (a.k.a. Expected P/E) is not provided, use the P/E which is based on the trailing last 12 months (TTM). Alternatively, calculate the E by using the E from P/E and multiplying it by its growth rate. It may not be seasonally adjusted. I prefer using Forward P/E as it provides a better predictability power to me.

  Finviz.com leaves the P/E blank (same as null) if the earnings are negative. In this case, I would check out Yahoo!Finance's EV / EBITDA, which also considers taxes, cash and interests. The blank condition is similar to some metrics such as when the asset is negative (they seldom occur).

Earnings Yield is equal to E/P. I call it True Earnings Yield for EBITDA / EV. It is easier to understand. Compare Earnings Yield or True Yield to the annual dividend yield of a 10-year Treasury – with the low interest rate in 2021, skip the comparison.

E/P is easier in screening and sorting the screened stocks. If you use P/E instead of E/P, you need to screen or sort stocks with a clause "P/E > 0".

When the P/E is less than 5, be careful and there may be a reason why it is so low. Many bankrupting companies have low P/Es at one time.

Compare the P/E or Forward P/E with the average P/E for the sector and its average P/E for the last 5 years that are available from Fidelity.com. Some sectors have high P/Es. If the sector is cyclical, the earnings could be affected.

When the prospect of the company is good such as Tesla in 2020, ignore P/E.

- **Cash / share**. It is used to calculate Pow P/E and Pow EY when EV/EBITDA for the stock is not available. To illustrate, if the stock is $10 and it has $10 cash / share without debt (i.e. Debt/Equity = 0), most likely it is underpriced as you can get the whole company for nothing. You should find out why the price is so low. It could be the market ignoring the stock, or there is a serious event happening such as a major lawsuit.

- **Dividend %** is useful for income investors. The payout ratio should not be more than 30% except for matured companies. Most developing companies plough back the profits into research and development, and hence they do not pay dividends.

- **Recs**. Select stocks with 1 or 2. Do not base your stock selection on this recommendation alone. There have been many bad recommendations that could cost you a fortune in losses. Use Fidelity's Equity Summary Score instead.

- **PEG** is a measure of the growth of P/E and hence a growth metric. It is similar to P/E, but it takes the expected earnings growth rate into account. The lower value is better as long as earnings are positive. If earnings are negative, then the reverse is true. It is a defect in using P/E and PEG and that's why I recommend EY (Earnings Yield) and EYG, earnings yield growth.

  If there are two companies with the same P/E, the one with a better PEG ratio is better. If two companies have the same E/P, the company with higher Earnings Growth (EPS Q/Q) would be better for similar logic.

- **P/B**. Book value (= Total Assets – Total Liabilities) may not include intangible assets such as patents. Do not trust it 100%, so is ROE which is based on the book value. Negative equity is possible when Total Liabilities is more than Total Assets. This popular metric is outdated for most matured companies as it is now made up of more intangible assets including patents, management, the quality of their employees, brand names, market share, partners, free cash flow and customer base.

- **P/S**. If two companies are unprofitable, this ratio can be used. A retail company such as Walmart is very different from a research company. This metric is only meaningful for stocks within the same sector or specific sectors.

- **P/FCF**. I prefer it to be greater than 0 and less than 50 for value investors. Most metrics can be manipulated easily, but not this one.

- **Sales Q/Q** reduces the seasonal deviation. To illustrate, retail sales for the Christmas season should be compared to the same season in the prior year.

- **EPS Q/Q**. Same as above. I prefer the growth of EPS over Sales. Both of these Q/Q ratios are growth metrics. When a company terminates its unprofitable product(s), its Sales Q/Q could be down but its EPS Q/Q could be up. In 2000, many internet companies had great Sales Q/Qs but negative EPS Q/Qs.

  Q/Q comparison (quarter to quarter) takes out the seasonal variations as Sales Q/Q. I prefer both Sales Q/Q and EPS Q/Q increase. When EPS

Q/Q increases far higher than Sales Q/Q, it could mean the EPS Q/Q could be temporary such as the oil company when the oil price rockets.

When the company buys its own shares, EPS could be misleading as E is fixed and the number of shares is reduced. In most cases, the fundamentals of the company have not changed.

- Positive **Insider** Transactions are favorable. Sometimes, they are misleading. Need to scroll to the end of the screen and check out more info there. If the transactions are outdated such as 3 months or so ago, and or they are purchases in a similar amount than the sales a while ago, they are not important. Insiders know the company better than us. So is Institutional Transactions as institutional investors move the market.

- Insider Own, Shares Outstanding and Shares **Float** determine the number of shares that are available for trading. A small Float with a high Insider Own limits trading and the stock should be avoided in most cases. Compare your trade position for the stock to the Avg. Volume.

- **Profit Margin**. I prefer it over Gross Margin and Oper. Margin which does not include interest expenses and taxes. When you sell software, the Gross Margin is high as it does not include development, support and marketing, etc. A retail store has low Gross Margin. It all depends on the industry, and hence it is better to compare companies in the same industry.

- **Short Float**. I prefer it to be less than 10%. If it is greater than 10%, the shorters could find something wrong with the company. If it is over 25% (indicating a possible short squeeze), I would check the fundamentals. If they are good, I would buy expecting a short squeeze potential. It is risky but it has been proven to be profitable for me.

- Technical metrics: SMA-20, SMA-50 and SMA-200. Finviz expresses them in convenient percentages. If they are all positive, it means the trend is up. SMA-20 and SMA-50 are a short-term trend and SMA-200 is a long-term trend. If you are a short-term swing investor, stick with the short-term trend and vice versa. The first two are also used as momentum grades. Many long-term investors do not buy stocks when the SMA-200% is negative.

- **RSI(14)**. If it is greater than 65%, it is overbought. If it is under 30%, it is under-bought for me. Some use 5% up or down than mine. Use it as a reference. Most stocks making new heights are always overbought, and many of these stocks keep on rising. I recommend using trailing stops to protect your profit.

- **Beta**. A volatile stock fluctuates a lot. It is good for short-term traders. A beta of 1 means the stock would fluctuate with the market, and be volatile if it is higher than 1. For volatile stocks (higher than 1), the stops should be higher. For example, if your stops are normally 15%, you may want to use 20% or even higher.

- Management performance is measured by **ROE**. It is also judged by **Analysts' Rec.** and Institutional Ownership (except for small companies). The confidence of their own ability, the company and its sector is measured by Insider Ownership and Insider Purchases.

    ROE = Net Income / Average Shareholder's Equity
    According to Investopedia, a normal ROE for utilities should be 10% while high tech companies should be 15%. Compare this ratio and many other ratios with its peers that are available from Fidelity.

- Avoid all companies that are going to bankrupt at all costs. Debt/Equity, P/FCF, Cash/Sh., P/B, Profit Margin, Forward P/E, Short Float, RSI(14), SMA20% and SMA50 would give us hints. Need to summarize all the info and study many other factors such as obsoleting products (including drugs).

- Unless you have concrete information, do not buy stocks a week or so before the Earnings Date. It is seldom to make great profits when the announcement is better than the expected.

More useful information:

- The price chart. It has a lot of features such as the resistance line. Some charts include technical indicators such as double top (a bearish warning) and double bottom (a bullish sign).
- Description under the symbol. It briefly describes what the company (sector and industry) does and its country of registration. You want to buy a stock within a sector that is trending up. For example, according

to Finviz Apple is in the Consumer Goods sector and the Electronic Equipment industry.

If you do not want to buy foreign stocks, skip it if it is not listed in the US exchange.
- Articles on the company for qualitative analysis.
- Insider trading. Pay more attention to the insider purchases at market prices. Use common sense.
- The last line lets you open Yahoo!Finance and other sites.

Other important sites

Yahoo!Finance.

From Statistics, you can find Enterprise Value / EBITDA. I call it True Yield when I flip them to EBITDA / Enterprise Value.

In case it is not available, I use Earnings Yield. In my spreadsheet without considering the cell designations,

=IF (Earnings Yield = "", True Yield, Earnings Yield)

Fidelity

Compare the P/E of the average PE of the last 5 years. In my spreadsheet for demonstration,

Cheaper By Historically =IF(PE="","",(Avg. of 5-year PE -PE)/Avg. of 5-year PE)

Compare the P/E of companies in the same sector. In my spreadsheet for demonstration,

Cheaper By To the peers =IF(PE="","",(Industry PE - PE)/Industry PE)

Your broker's website

Your broker website should have plenty of tools to analyze stocks. As of Dec., 2018, Fidelity lets you use their extensive research free by opening an account with no position restriction. I describe some of their metrics that should be beneficial to your research.

- Equity Summary Score. Potentially good buy when it is 7 (8 for conservative investors) or higher. With some exceptions, you should avoid or short stocks if the score is 3 or below. The stocks ranking from 4 to 6 could be turnaround candidates if they are supported by good Q/Q Earnings and/or good news.

- The 5-year averages are good yardsticks. For example, in Dec., 2018, C's P/E is about 9 and the average is 14. Hence it is a value buy.

Other sources

If you have other sources (most require a subscription or being a customer), skip the stocks that have one of the failing grades. The exceptions are a new positive development and increased insider purchases.

Vendor	Grade	Fail
Fidelity	Equity Summary Score	< 7
IBD	Composite grade	< 50
Value Line	Proj. 3-5 yr. return. Also its composite rating	< 3%
Zacks	Rank	5
VectorVest	VST	< 0.7

You may be able to find Value Line and IBD in your library. Try out the free stock reports from your broker first. Finviz and Seeking Alpha should have articles (now fewer free articles from Seeking Alpha) on stocks and earnings conferences, which could have important information after separating from the "welcome" and garbage talks.

Yahoo!Finance has good info. "EV/EBITDA" is better than "P/E" as it considers debts and cash. Most use Earnings from last 12 months, which has poorer predictability than Forward Earnings to me.

When negative values such as Equity in Finviz.com, we need to adjust many related metrics or do not use them at all.

MarketWatch.com has many articles on the market in general and personal investing.

If the stock is close to the Earnings Date (found in Finviz.com), you should avoid trading the stock; as earnings could have a big swing for the stock price. Consult Zacks' ranking which is currently free for individual stocks.

Gurus

It is nice to know how gurus would rate the interested stocks. GuruFocus is a good source. NASDAQ is a simplified version, but it is currently free. Bring up Nasdaq.com from your browser. Select "Investing" and then "Guru Screeners". On the third selection, enter the stock symbol such as THO. Click "Go". You will find how 10 or so gurus would evaluate this stock in theory. Click "Detailed Analysis" for each guru.

Quick and dirty

Many times we need to evaluate a stock fast such as taking action due to some development. Refer to my other article "Simplest way to evaluate stocks". The following should take a few minutes. Bring up Finviz.com and enter the stock symbol.

Using SWKS on 6/10/16 to illustrate, Forward P/E is about 11 (fine between 3 and 25), Debt/Eq. is 0 (fine less than .5), ROE is 30% (fine greater than 5%) and P/PCF is 31 (fine if not negative).

Also, check out Market Cap, Avg. Volume, Dividend, Short Float (fine between 0% and 10%), Country and Industry. Judging from the above, it is a buy.

If you have more time, check out the following: Recom. (Ok if less than 2.5), P/B (fine between .5 and 4), Sales Q/Q (fine if not negative), EPS Q/Q (fine if not negative), Cash/Sh (compare it to Debt/Sh) and Profit Margin (fine >5%). Check some articles described for this stock.

5-minute stock evaluation

It takes even less time than the above "Quick and Dirty". However, I recommend you should spend more time researching stocks.

- From Finviz.com, enter the stock or ETF symbol. Look at the number of reds in metrics. If there are more than greens, most likely it is not a good stock.

- It should be fine if Fidelity's Equity Summary Score is greater than 8.

If you have more time, I recommend you to check the following:

- Check out Forward P/E (E>0 and P/E < 20), Debut / Equity (< 50%) and P/FCF (not in red color).

  If time is allowed, replace Forward P/E with True P/E (same as "EV/EBITDA"), which is available from Yahoo!Finance and other sources.

- SMA20 (or SMA50 for longer holding period). If SMA20 is > 10%, it is trending up.

- It is fine if the Insider Transaction is positive.

- Be cautious on foreign stocks and low-volume stocks.

- If most of the above are positive, it is likely a buy. As in life, nothing is 100% certain.

Links
PEG: http://en.wikipedia.org/wiki/PEG_ratio
Short %: http://www.investopedia.com/university/shortselling/shortselling1.asp#axzz2LNDvpemo
Openinsider: http://www.openinsider.com/
Finviz: http://Finviz.com/
terms: http://www.Finviz.com/help/screener.ashx
Insider Cow: http://www.insidercow.com/
Current Ratio: http://en.wikipedia.org/wiki/Current_ratio
How to find quality stocks.
http://seekingalpha.com/article/2381395-how-to-identify-quality-stocks-and-is-there-really-alpha-to-be-had

3   Intangibles

I give a score for each stock I evaluate. Occasionally some stocks with poor scores have great returns and vice versa. In general, the scoring system works. It has been proven statistically and repeatedly from my limited data. I stick with high-score stocks with some exceptions.

Once in a while I change my scoring system to adept to the current market conditions. To illustrate, the market bottom phase and early recovery phase of the market cycle favor value more than momentum/growth. Here are some of my recent experiences and strategies:

- I double or even triple my stake on stocks with high scores. In the longer term, they are consistently better winners than the average with some minor exceptions. Besides the score, look at the intangibles described in this article.

- Watch out for the stocks with outrageous metrics such as P/E of 4 or less. It could be a big lawsuit pending, an expiration of some important drugs, etc. Also, be careful with scores in the top 5%. From my statistics they do worse than the average. Their problems may not show up in the current financial statements.

- The technology of a tech company cannot be ignored even though the company's P/E is high, that I set a limit of 25 instead of 20 for other stocks. The value of the company's technology and patents will not be shown in the fundamental metrics except from the insiders' purchases at market prices.

  For example, IDCC rose about 40% in 2 days. There was a rumor that Google was buying the company and/or Apple was bidding on it too for its mobile technology. Charts usually would flag this kind of event. For non-charters, use the SMA-20% from Finviz.com. They could be a little late as the charts depend on rising prices.

- There are more acquisitions during a market bottom (same as early recovery). The companies with good technologies are bargains and the larger companies especially those in the same sector understand their values better than most of us. These potentially profitable companies will not be shown by their scores explicitly. When corporations have a lot of cash or the credit is cheap, they are looking for smaller companies to acquire or invest in. The candidates are usually small, beaten up, low-priced and having valuable intangible assets such as technologies, customer base and/or market share of the industry segment. 2009-2012 was just the perfect environment and the before that was 2003. I had at least one stock in each of these periods and they appreciated a lot.

- The opposite is Netflix, Chipotle in 1/2012 and Amazon in 1/2013. They are over-priced by any measure. However, the mentioned companies are investing in the future. The shorters (not for beginners) are having a tough time in making money on them. When their P/Es are higher than 40, watch out. Some could be OK in the mentioned companies, but usually they are not. Do not follow the herd and your due diligence will verify whether they will still go up.

  Use reward/risk ratio. It is based on experiences. To illustrate, if the company has the equal chance to go up 50% and go down 25%, then it is a buy and the reverse is a sell.

- The retail investor just cannot possibly know about some events until they actually happen. For example, ATSC dropped 15% due to losing its second primary customer. Fundamentals cannot predict this kind of events. Charts can signal this event, but usually they are too late unless you watch the chart all day long.

- After a quick run up, TZOO plunged due to missing some negligible earning expectations. It seems the original climbing prices already had the perfect earnings growth built-in.

  I do not understand why a company loses 10% of its market cap when it missed by 1% of the expected earnings. It could be driven up and down by the institutional investors. Evaluate the stock before you act. Acting opposite to the institutional investors could be very profitable for the right stocks. Avoid trading before the earnings announcement dates (about 4 times a year for most stocks).

- The following are not easily found in financial statements: industry outlook, patents, good will, market share, competition, product margins, management quality, lawsuits pending, potential acquisition, pension obligations, advertising icons, etc. That is why we need to read articles on the stocks in our buy list or our purchased stocks.

- The financial data could be fraudulent or manipulated. I do not trust small companies in emerging markets. I have been burned too many times. Check the company names such as foreign names, ADR and their headquarter addresses (from the company profile in most investing sites).

  Earnings can be manipulated with many accounting tricks. A jump in earnings from last year may not be as rosy as it looks. Check the footnotes in the accounting statements. I usually skip financial statements unless I have big purchases in mind as my time in investing is limited.

- Cash flow cannot be easily manipulated. It is good information whether the company will survive or not, but to me it does not prove to be a consistent predictor in my tests, but an important red flag for companies on their way to bankruptcy. Examples abound.

- Repeated one-time, non-recurring and extraordinary charges are red flags.

- Stay away from the companies where the CEOs are over-compensated. As of 7- 2013, Activision's CEO raised his salary by more than 600%, while the stock lost its value in double digits.

- Value stocks. Need to know why they become value stocks (i.e. fewer investors want to own) even they are financially sound. For example, there are two primary reasons for the downfall of a supplier to Apple: 1. Apple is declining in sales and 2. Apple is switching suppliers to replace their product. Technology companies are continually building better mouse traps. They could turn around in a year or so with better products.

Conclusion

Buying a stock is an educated guess that its stock price will rise. Fundamentals do not always work, but they work most of the time:

1. When we buy a value stock, we're swimming against the tide. Hence, we need to wait longer (usually more than 6 months) for the market to realize its value. The exception is the Early Recovery phase (see the

Market Cycle chapter) and it has faster and larger returns than most other stocks from most other stages of the market cycle.

2. Some metrics are misleading. Book value could be misleading for an established company such as IBM. The image of the cowboy in a tobacco company could be a very important asset that is not included in its financial statement.

3. The market is not always rational.

Afterthoughts

- Brand names of big companies are one of the most important intangibles. Here is a strategy to buy big companies in a down market. It has been proven that it works. However, do not just buy these companies without analysis.
http://seekingalpha.com/article/1324041-buying-brand-names-in-a-bear-market-can-make-you-rich

- The reputation of a company takes a long time to build but a bad incidence to destroy in the case of GM such as the delay in recalling the killer switches.

## 4	Qualitative analysis

This is the last analysis to evaluate a stock fundamentally. Then the next is technical analysis which is used to find an entry point (also the exit point) for the stock.

Where quantitative analysis fails and why

I find that some stocks with high scores fail and some stocks with low scores succeed as indicated by my performance monitor. The scoring system still works statistically for the majority of my stocks.

- Reasons why stocks with low scores perform in addition to the described in the last discussion:

    o Over-sold. The institutional investors (fund managers and pension managers) dump them first, and then followed by the retail investors. These big boys will buy these stocks back when they reach a certain price range. RSI(14), a technical indicator described in the Technical Analysis article, is useful to detect these over-sold stocks. This metric is readily available from many sites including Finviz.

    o The falling price (P) improves all fundamental metrics that have the stock price such as P/E and P/Sales. However, the trend of the price is down.

    o The company has turned around after fixing its problems and/or the market has changed for the better.

    o The current problems have been resolved but not known to the public. It includes resolving a lawsuit, a new product, a new drug, or a new big order, etc.

    o Heavy purchases by insiders. The company's outlook is not shown in its financial statements. Sometimes the insiders hide them so they can buy more of their companies' stocks for themselves.

- Reasons why stocks with high scores plunge in addition to the described in the previous discussion:

- The company's fundamentals and its prices have reached or closed to the maximum heights. They have no way to go but down. It is particularly true when the stock's timing rating is at or close to the highest point. TTWO that I gifted to my grandchildren had been 5-baggers in the last few years before it plunged in 2018.

- It has reached its potential value (or a target price) and it is time for many investors to take profits.

- Sector (or stock) rotation, particularly by institutional investors who drive the market.

- The outlook of the company, its sector and/or the market is deteriorating.

- The stock price may be manipulated. There are many reasons to pump and dump the stock. Shorting is not recommended for most investors. However, some experienced shorters make money consistently when they find valid reasons to short stocks.

- It could be due to a new serious lawsuit, a new competing product or drug, canceling a major order, etc.

- Downgrade by analysts. They could spot some bad events such as product defects, violations of regulations or accounting errors / frauds. The downgrades are more important than the upgrades that could have conflict of interest.

- The financial statement had been manipulated. The SEC may ask for an investigation.

- Does not meet the consensus in earnings announcements, which have been over-acted by many investors.

Qualitative Analysis

We need to do further analysis after the quantitative analysis and the intangible analysis. Check out the company's prospects. Check out the date of the article and any potential hidden agenda items from the author. Older articles may not have much value.

Be careful on 'pump-and-dump' manipulation written by authors with a hidden agenda. It has happened especially on small companies before even SeekingAlpha.com has its share. Here was an article that tells you to sell NHTC. There was another article to tell you to buy ARTX. They fit into this category.

The sources are:

1. Seeking Alpha.
    Type the symbol of the company to read as many articles on the company as you have time for. Today this site and many other similar sites require you to be a paid member. If you cannot find too many good articles, check out the articles from Finviz.com.

    Recently, I read an article on AMD and it said it may have good profits in the next two years with the game consoles. The outlook of a company is not shown by any fundamental metric which are far from favorable.

    Following a well-known writer, I bought IBM without doing my due diligence (my fault). It went down more than 15% quickly. You can learn from my mistakes.

2. Research reports from your broker. If you do not find many, open an account with one that provides such reports. Some subscription services such as Value Line provide such reports.

3. Yahoo!Finance board. Most comments are garbage. However, once in a while you find some great insights. Usually you cannot find any info from other sources on tiny companies.

4. The most recent company's financial statements. They are usually available in the company's web site.

5. 10-Ks from Edgar database (www.sec.gov/edgar). Check out new products and its potential competition, key customers, order backlog, research and development and pending lawsuits.

6. Check out the outlook of the sector the company is in and the company itself.

7. Check out its competitors.

8. Some companies are run by stupid people. I received information via my email saying that my mutual fund account could be treated as an abandoned property. I have been cashing dividend checks every year and why it would be considered as an abandoned property. I called them right away to close my account.

   The tall and handsome guy presented articulately how he would turn around JC Penny on TV. I could tell you right away that all his tricks had been tried by other companies such as Sears, and most did not work. The intelligent investor does not care about how handsome, how articulated, how rich his family is and how many advanced degrees from prestigious colleges he possesses. If he does not make sense, do not buy his preaching and his company's stock. [Update. As of 5/2020, J.C. Penny filed for bankruptcy protection. If you had this stock and my book, you would have saved a lot of money minus $10 for my book!]

9. Check out its business model. Some business models do not make business sense and some do. Here are some samples.

- Giving razors makes sense, as the customers have to buy the blades eventually and keep on buying blades for life.

- Supermarket M lowers prices on common merchandises such as Coke and it works. They make money by providing inferior (but profitable to them) products that you cannot compare prices easily such as meat and seafood.

  Eventually there will be a supermarket in my area to satisfy me both in price and quality or at least make a good tradeoff.
- Last week it had been brutally hot. I went to a Barns & Noble's bookstore to enjoy reading the updated books and enjoyed the air conditioning. When there are more free loaders like me than customers, this business model does not work.
- Market dumping works to capture the market. Microsoft used to do it with their new Office and Mail products that could not compete with the established products at the time. Google is following the same model to dump its equivalent products to compete with Office. Now, Microsoft is taking a dose of the same medicine.

5   Avoid bankrupting companies

Avoid the bankrupting companies at all costs. Here are some hints that a company is going bankrupt:

- I had several companies that had lost most of their stock values. It turns out that most were Chinese companies. I did have some losers from Mexico, Israel and Ireland. I believe most were set up to cheat investors. Most if not all had 'rosy' financial statements. Avoid them, especially small companies in emerging countries.
- Many U.S. companies failed due to fraud, poor management, and/or the management betting wrongly. When the CEO is using the company as his own AMT, or having an extravagant life style, watch out. If they promise you a return doubling the current rate of return of the market, listen to your wise mother: there is no free lunch. Despite so many real examples, still fools are born every day, because greed is a human nature.
- Do not follow the 'commentators' on TV. They have their own hidden agenda which usually is not in your interest.
- Many companies fail due to their lack of ability to pay back their loans. Except for specific industries and situations, avoid companies with high debt (Debt/Equity over 50%). Financial institutions and companies that have high debt in order to finance their products for their customers such as utilities are the exceptions.
- I have a screen named Big Losers beating the market by more than 600% in Early Recovery (a phase defined by me). However, some bankrupted companies are not included in the database which is termed as survivor bias. Hence, the actual result is far worse than the 600%. I still use this screen but skip these companies using the following yardsticks.
    - The companies are usually safe with high Free Cash Flow / Equity and high Expected Profit / Stock Price.
    - The following are red flags: low Free Cash Flow / Equity, high Inventory and high Receivable (esp. relative to its Payable), high P/B (over 30) and high net Debt/Equity (over 1 to 3 depending on the industry).
    - P/PFC should be greater than 0 and less than 50. A healthy cash flow may not be able to service the debt if it is too huge. Hence, compare it to Debt/Equity. Compare the cash flow per year to debt obligations per year.
- New government regulations could bankrupt an industry. What would happen when the U.S. takes out the rebates and subsidies of solar

panels? When the U.S. banned solar panels from China, one of my Chinese stocks went bankrupt. Also government bailed out bankrupting companies such as Chrysler (that I made a good profit) and AIG Fannie Mae in 2008.

- Serious lawsuits- Most U.S. companies are required to file this information in their financial reports.
- Obsolete products. Newspapers, retail and similar products would be replaced by the internet. The opposite is new products such as virtual reality products.
- Many companies run out of money during the development phase of the major products. Many are too optimistic in their business plans.
- If you expect the market will recover in 2 years, ensure the company's cash and net income can support their burn rate for at least two more years.
- Many investing sites (most require subscriptions) have safety scores.
- If the Beneish M-Score is greater than -2.22, the company is likely an accounting manipulator.
- Choose companies with Z-Score higher than 3; it does not applicable to financial companies. Both M-Score and Z-Score are available from GuruFocus, a paid subscription. Z-Score does not work for financial institutions.
- Z-Score metrics are: "Working Capital / Total Assets" (A), "Retained Earnings / Total Assets" (B), "Earnings Before Interest & Taxes / Total Assets" (C), "Market Cap / Total Liabilities" (D) and "Sales / Total Assets" (E).
Z-Score = 1.2 A + 1.4 B + 3.3 C + .6 D + E
- Market timing- It does not always work, but it is far better to follow a proven technique than not. It is far safer to take money out of the market when the market is too risky or is plunging. The big losers are companies that provide non-essential products in a down turn.
- Small companies could be risky but very profitable. Typically they have a low stock price (less than $5), small market cap (less than 50 M), low sales (less than $25 M) and low institutional ownership (less than 5%).
- Avoid companies when their own bond ratings are not equal to AAA or AA (www.moodys.com).
- The fall of a sector such as oil in 2015 could drive the related companies, or even a country to the brink of bankruptcy.

Investing is risky to start with. However, investing especially in stocks has been proven to be the best vehicle to beat inflation.

6   Should you hold stocks forever?

There are many examples that you should hold onto some stocks forever such as Apple, Netflix, Amazon and Google. Interestingly there are more opposite examples such as AIG and Lehman Brothers. Hence, there is no right or wrong answer. Always continually monitor your stock holdings and the sectors they are in.

Even IBM could suffer its dips when it does not react to its market and / or make the wrong strategic decision. The Washington Post has to react to the free articles from the internet.

I have set up guidelines on when to sell. One selling indicator is when those shares lose over 25%. We have to admit that we have made a mistake, or the fundamentals of the stock have changed. Evaluate the fundamentals of the purchased stocks periodically.

Boston Chicken is one of my many big losers. I could use the money I lost to have chicken dinner every night for the rest of my life! This kind of thinking is not healthy. I decided not to buy any restaurant stock again and that is not rational either. It is an art to sell a loser, or wait for its potential recovery. From my experiences, it is better to sell the loser.

If you have a historical database, you can test out your strategy on when to sell and adjust the sell criteria accordingly. Do not try to data fit to your strategy.

Never fall in love in a stock and never be afraid to buy back a sold stock. Use fundamental metrics for making a buy/sell decision.

Taxes and diversification

Tax should not be a major consideration in selling a stock. However, you may postpone selling losers in December if your tax rate (so your tax loss value) will be better next year. If you need to offset short-term capital gains, sell some losers eligible for short-term capital losses. Postpone selling a winner to a month or so, if it can be eligible for long-term capital gain.

When your stock appreciates many, many times and you're close to your life expectant age, hold it and the cost basis will step up to the day you pass away. Instruct your heirs to buy a newspaper to get the prices of your stocks you hold or instruct your heirs to inform your broker on the unavoidable day. Today's tax law provides a range of days around the date of death; check the current tax laws.

Instead of selling a stock with huge gain, consider options: 1. give it to your children who have lower tax brackets, 2. give it to charity, and 3. save it for your estate.

When the market is plunging as detected by market timing techniques, sell most of your holdings. Be warned that market timing does not always work.

No stock is sacred

That's why we need to churn the portfolio replacing the bad stocks with better ones. More examples of failing companies that had been very promising at one time:

- The bankrupt companies due to competition: Circuit City (due to BestBuy) and Block Buster (due to Netflix).
- The failing internet companies in 2000 and the financial institutions in 2008.
- HP when PCs, servers and printers are no longer kings.
- BestBuy killed Circuit City and then it is being eaten alive by Amazon, Walmart, Costco and BJ. However, it recovered in 2014.
- Many retailers went bankrupt. I lost count of so many of the retailers in the Boston area alone.

Filler: Dream high

I heard this. The girl wanted to be a president when she grew up. She went to a circus and she said she wanted to be a clown. Her wise father said, "You can be a president and a clown at the same time". Reality?

Should we modify the Constitution to ban our presidents from twitting especially in the private places?

It is a laughing stock for injecting disinfectant to cure the virus. At least we fix the racial discrimination when everyone has been bleached.

I am neutral in politics. I complained a lot on Obama.

7 When to sell a stock

There are many reasons to sell a stock as follows.

Personal

1. Has met my targets/objectives.
   It could be a 10% gain in a very short-term swing, x% return in 4 months for a short-term swing or y% gain after a year for long-term trades. Define x and y depending on your risk tolerance and how often you trade.

   I bought 4 stocks in one day during the August, 2015 correction and placed sell orders with 10% more than my purchase prices. I sold one in a day and another one within a month. This is my strategy for correction – sometimes it works and sometimes it does not.

   Never look back. Do not blame yourself when the prices are better than your trade prices. When the market is volatile, use a higher percent of the current prices. Be disciplined. Stay on the same strategy and detach yourself from emotions.

2. Realize that we have made a mistake. Do not let your ego block your eyes. It could be due to bad analysis, bad, data, unexpected fraud, lawsuits, and/or unforeseeable events that you have no control of. It is better to get out with a small loss. I prefer a 25% loss as a threshold for long-term strategies and a 10% (or less for some strategies) loss for short-term strategies.

   We have to ensure whether it is a mistake or not. If the 'mistake' is just bad luck or due to conditions we cannot possibly predict or control, then it is not a mistake. If it is a mistake, learn from it. When we diversify, one bad loss should not cause a big dent in our portfolios. The stop loss is a good tool most of the time except when there is a flash crash.

   If the criteria have been faithfully followed and it does not work well, check out whether your criteria are wrong, or it does not work on the current market conditions.

3. When we have too many stocks in the same sector, we will want to replace some stocks to better diversify our portfolios.

   When the sector is rising, we want to weigh more on that sector at the expense of diversification, and vice versa. Set a limit of how many sectors you should hold.

4. Need cash for living expenses.

5. To reduce a tax burden by selling some losers. Tax consideration should not be the primary reason for selling. Take advantage of the favorable tax treatment for long-term capital gains. In short, sell losers within the short term limit (currently a year), and sell winners after 365 days; check the current tax laws.

   Harvest tax losses. Sell losers and buy back similar stocks (or same stock after 31 days to avoid wash sale). It is not too clear in which you can buy back the same loser in your children's account under the current tax law.

6. To take advantage of a lower tax. In 2013, we can pay virtually zero (except the increase of tax on social security payment) Federal income taxes on long-term capital gains when our income is below a specific tax bracket (15% as of 2015). Check out the current tax laws. Evaluate the sold winners for a possible buy back.

Market Timing

7. When the market or the sector plunges, sell stocks or stocks within the sector.

   For temporary peaks, evaluate which stocks in your portfolio to sell based on fundamentals. The objective is to raise cash for buying opportunities.

Deteriorating appreciation potential

8. There may be some stocks that have a better appreciation potential than the ones you currently own. Churning the portfolio by replacing better stocks may cost some brokerage commissions (some are free

today) and taxes for taxable accounts, but it improves the quality and the appreciation potential for the entire portfolio.

9. The company's fundamentals have changed for the worse. If you use a scoring system, compare the current score with the score you actually bought the stock for. Apple is a good example from 2013 to 2015. Buy when the fundamentals are good and sell when they are not.

The basic fundamentals are expected P/E, the quarter-to-quarter earnings growth rate / the sales growth rate, and Debt /Equity.

When your stocks have passed the peak and started to decline, sell them. When they are heading to bankruptcy, sell them fast.

Hints that the fundamentals are degrading

Evaluate the stocks you own at least every 6 months and check their daily news at least once a week that can be easily done using Seeking Alpha's portfolio function.

- The cash flow is decreasing fast. Cash flow is not a particularly good predicative indicator for appreciation, but a good indicator on whether the company will survive. This metric is very hard to manipulate.

- A new or pending lawsuit. Check out how serious the lawsuit is and be aware that a minor lawsuit can be ignored. Companies always sue against each other.

- A big drop in sales. Do not be alarmed when a new product, or a new drug is going to replace a major product. Compare sales to the same quarter of prior year to avoid seasonal fluctuations (Q-to-Q info I available from Finviz.com).

- Management deteriorates- One hint is the deteriorating ROE from the last quarter.

- The extravagant life style of the CEO and the many easy loans to officers.

- Poor operations. They include recalls of products such as the GM recall on ignition switches, product secrets being stolen and customers' credit card info being stolen. Boeing's 747-Max is a warning call.

- A successful product from the competitor, or the current product is losing its market share, or becoming a low-profit commodity.

- Insiders and/or institutional investors are dumping the companies' stocks far more than the averages (2% for me) especially in heavy volumes and by more than one insider.

    - Have more than one insider dumping a lot of the stock within a month and no insider purchase in that month.

    - Have more than one insider decrease their holdings by more than 10%.

- When the SEC or any government agency pays attention to a company, it usually means bad news.

- Deceptive accounting practices have been discovered.

- Increasing receivable and/or inventory at an alarming rate.

- Earnings have been restated too many times.

- Short percentage is increasing fast – someone found something wrong with the company.

- The invalidity of 'one-time charges'.

- Abnormal return rate of the company's pension fund comparing to the average of the companies in the same sector.

- Too many and too costly reconstructing charges.

- The entire stock market is plunging as indicated by our chart in detecting market crashes.

- The stock price does not move up with good news. It shows the price has peaked.

- The accumulation amount is far less than the sold amount. When the stock price is up, the accumulation is less than the sold stocks when the stock price was down the last time. It indicates that no more accumulation is ahead and hence the stock will be down most likely.

Afterthoughts

- Another article on this topic.
  http://buzz.money.cnn.com/2013/04/05/stocks-sell/
  An article from Investopedia. Nothing new but it is worth having the same second opinion.
  http://www.investopedia.com/financial-edge/0412/5-tips-on-when-to-sell-your-stock.aspx

- It also depends on your strategies. I sell most of my stocks in my momentum portfolio within a month. At least one strategy I know of does not keep any stock during the peak stage of the market cycle – the easiest time to make money but also the riskiest time.

  If you use charts for trading, sell the stocks that are below your moving averages or other technical analysis indicators. Personally I do not use charts for making sell decisions due to my limited time.

- Sell when the company is heading into bankruptcy as described before. The red flags are: 1. Negative cash flow. 2. Heavy insiders dumping the stocks. 3. Pending major lawsuit. 4. Fraud from the management.

- Risky periods for a stock.
  Earnings announcement (4 times a year), settling a major lawsuit and/or during a FDA event in approving a drug are risky periods for a stock. A fluctuation more than 5% in either direction is normal. Some use options to buy insurance. Most ignore it. For the majority of the time, heavy insider purchase is a good indicator. There are rumors (or educated guesses) on earnings before their announcements. Zacks is supposed to be a good subscription for earnings estimates.

8 Selling a winner

Let the profit rise and at the same time protect your profit. Tesla quadrupled its value in 6 months. Examples abound such as Amazon and Yelp.

You do not want to sell these rocket stocks even if their fundamentals do not make sense. Buffett does not touch these stocks and he usually misses these big gains. However, many of these rocket stocks such as BRRY (Blackberry) will eventually fall losing most of their value. I bet the institutional investors move the market in either direction and usually they read the same analysts' reports. You profit as a contrarian if you have a good reason to act against the herd.

The following example uses a 10% trailing stop. Set the stop at 10% of the current price (i.e. 10% less than the current price), not the purchase price. You need to change the stop when the price rises but do not change it when the price falls. Review your stops every month or more frequently if time allows.

To illustrate, when the stock price rises to 100, set the stop at 90. When the stock price falls to 90, sell the stock at the market price. When the stock price rises to 200, change the stop at 180.

The stop should also be set according to how volatile the stock is. Some stocks are more volatile than others. Most charts show the resistance line. This line assumes the stock price should not fall below this line in normal fluctuations. Set the stop at 2% below this line so your stock will not be stopped out in theory.

To avoid flash crashes, do not place stop orders. Instead, do it mentally (mental stop is my term). When you see that the stock falls below your stop with no sign of a flash crash, sell the stock using a market order.

Of course, there is no bullet-proof scheme. This one should work in the long run. This is my suggestion only, so examine whether it works for you. Small cap and/or stocks with small average volumes fluctuate more.

Examples
I have too many bad examples of selling the stocks too early and sometimes holding them too long.

I made over 40% in a few weeks on ALU, but it went up more than 300% in the next two years. It was acquired in early 2016 by Nokia paying a good premium. I was right that ALU had a lot of valuable patents and I was wrong to dump it when I found out Cisco did not have any intention to acquire it – a big mistake by Cisco and the U.S.

FOSL is another example to teach us to use mental stop loss. FOSL was priced at $33.70 on 1/4/2010. Its fundamentals were just fine with an expected E/P (expected earnings yield) at 6% but decreasing earnings. It gained 115% later in 2010 - not expected.

On 1/3/2011, the expected E/P was still at around 6% and improving earnings. It gained 9% for the year – a little disappointing.

On 1/3/2012, the expected E/P was 7% and a huge earnings growth. Now, we expected a better performance for the year and it did by gaining 20%.

On 1/3/2013, the expected E/P was about 6% and the earnings gain was respectable. It gained 28% to $121. So far, so good.

On 1/2/2014, the E/P and the earnings growth were about the same as in 1/3/2013. However, it lost 7% for the year while SPY (an ETF simulating the market) gained 12%. There was no warning. Did the institutional investors lose the interest of this stock?

On 1/2/2015, the E/P was 7% and the earnings growth was about the same as the previous year. It lost 69% (vs. SPY's 0% return with dividends)!

From 1/4/2010 to 1/3/2016, the annualized return of FOSL is 0% (vs. SPY's 13%). Actually, after dividends, SPY should have an annualized return of about 15%. The lessons gained here are:

- Fundamentals (using EP and earnings growth in this example) may not always work. Otherwise, 2015 should have the same gain as 2014.

- The rosy outlook of the stock may be priced in already. When the outlook fails to materialize, the stock tanks.

9   Examples of over-priced stocks

In 2011, there were discussions on the high valuation of Netflix in several articles in Seeking Alpha, an investment website. LinkedIn and Facebook shares were believed to be overvalued even before their IPOs.

Here are some of my thoughts on Netflix and the same concept can be applied to other stocks.

- Reward / Risk ratio.
  If the stock has the same probability to move up by 30% and move down by 50%, it is overvalued by 20% (50% - 30%). As of 2011, Netflix shares may rise, but it is too risky for me.
- Compare the P/E to its five-year average.
  The current P/E is 60 and the average for the last 5 years is 30. From this metric it is overvalued by 100%.

  The 'E' in P/E can be either expected (same as forward) earnings or based on the last 12 months (same as trailing or historical). It has been proven that the 'expected' is a better indicator than the 'historical'. AAII demonstrated this by comparing the performances of the expected PEG screen and the historical PEG screens over a long period of time.
- Fools who invested in the high P/E stocks and did not do their due diligence in 2000 had parted with their money fast. I could not convince my friends to take money off their internet stocks. It is similar to asking the lottery winners not to buy lottery tickets.
- Buying an expensive stock is like over paying for a hot dog cart in NYC for $100,000. The buyer will sell many hot dogs, but the rate of return of the investment will be minimal, and it will never recover the initial investment. "Buy high and sell higher" is a momentum play. It works if it is played with stops, but I prefer to "Buy low and sell high".
- Following a decent and proven investing strategy consistently should lead to success through persistence and adjustments. In the long term, a bad strategy always loses money.
- When the market favors growth / momentum (vs. value), it is OK to buy stocks with prices higher than the intrinsic values by a small percentage. The tide is on your side. However, be attentive to any indication that the market is changing direction. NFLX has an average annual return rate of 177% vs. SPY's 14% from 1/3/2011 to 1/3/2020 without considering dividends. Hence, a trailing stop would do the job for the rocket stock.

10 Technical analysis (TA)

The basics

Technical analysis (a.k.a. charting) is easier to learn than you might expect. It represents the trend of the market (a stock or a group of stocks) graphically. If more investors are in the market, the market would move upwards until it changes direction. We divide the trends into short-term, intermediate-term and long-term.

The chartists usually do not consider fundamentals as they believe they have already been priced into the stock price and some fundamentals are not available to the public. To illustrate, a new drug has been discovered, the stock price of the company jumps initially by insiders purchases and the informed. Its fundamental metrics do not demonstrate this right away, but many investors are buying to boost up the stock price as evidenced by the technical indicators such as SMA for 20 or 50 days.

The volume is a confirmation. When the stock moves up or down by 10% with a low volume, the trend is not yet confirmed.

The trend of the stock price is not a straight line in most cases. Hence a trend line is usually drawn to indicate the direction of the stock. Many investors believe the stocks fluctuate in certain ranges (i.e. channels) and the chart draws the upper value (the resistance line) and the lower value (the support line). In theory, the price of a stock fluctuates within the resistance line (ceiling for understanding) and support (floor). When it reaches its support, it becomes a buy and vice versa for a sell. Most charts including Finviz.com would display these lines.

When the price passes out of the channel, it is called a breakout. Darvas, one of the oldest and most successful chartists, profited from the breakouts of the resistance line and believed the stock was close to the support line of the new channel. Hence it would be a long way up in theory.

If it were so simple, there will be no poor folks

It works most of the time, but do not place all your money on it. For chartists, 51% is great (the same for playing Black Jack). Some trends reverse very fast such as the bio drug stocks in 2015. You need to hedge your bets such as placing stop orders. Most do not want to spend their lives in watching the trend from a big screen.

Most novices use too many technical indicators and lose in their performances to the professionals. Recently, most chartists were not doing all that great and I did not find many books on their success than a decade ago. It could be due to too many followers in similar setups. I verified it with my recent testing using Finviz.com.

Simple Moving Average

The basic technical indicator is SMA-N. It is the average of the last N trade sessions. When N is 20 (or SMA-20), we classify it as short-term. Similarly, SMA-50 is an intermediate-term and SMA-200 is long-term. I prefer 50, 100 and 250. This trend duration is important. For example, do not want to place long-term purchases using the short-term SMA-50. There are many modifications to SMA such as giving more weight to recent data, but I have not found them any better. Finviz.com includes this information without charting (SMA-20, SMA-50 and SMA-100 in percentages).

Defining the trend periods is rather arbitrary. I use SMA-350 to detect the market plunges and SMA-100 for stocks. Weighted Moving Average weighs more weight on recent price data.

It can be used to determine whether we are in bull, bear or a sideways market using SMA-50 (or SMA-200 for longer term) for the market (using SPY), the sector (using an ETF for the sector and the specific stock. The trend is up when it the price is above the SMA and the reversal of the trend.

https://www.youtube.com/watch?v=jdYNaE5GJ0k&list=WL&index=5&t=609s

The trend is your best friend
Most traders use TA for trending in a short duration. Investors can also use TA to time the entry and exit points for better potential profits. Value investors usually are patient and they do bottom fishing and they search for 'oversold' condition using RSI(14). Again high volume is a confirmation.

Many sites provide charting free of charge such as Yahoo!Finance. Finviz.com provides a lot of technical indicators without charting such as SMA% and RSI(14). It also provides screen searching for stocks that meet your technical analysis criteria.

Hands on

Bring up Finviz.com and enter any stock symbol such as AAPL. You can see the daily prices of AAPL from about nine months ago to today. Three SMAs (Simple Moving Average) are displayed as SMA-20, SMA-50 and SMA-200. The first two are for short-term trends. When the price is above the SMA, it is expected to be trending up. Again, the trade volume is used as a confirmation.

You can also see the resistance line and the support line drawn. In theory, the stock will trade within these lines. When it exceeds its resistance line, it is called a breakout, and vice versa for a breakdown. Sometimes it displays some technical patterns such as Cup and Shoulder and Double Down (both are positive patterns).

Select Weekly data. The Candle chart is better described than the Daily chart. Candles give us better descriptions of the price: open, close, high and low. The green color indicates the price is up for the period (a week in this example) and the red color indicates a down period.

In addition, Finviz.com includes some technical indicators in the metric section such as RSI. Most other chart sites are similar in the basics. Use Finviz's Help and select Technical Analysis for more description. Investopedia has enhanced descriptions on this topic.

TA patterns

There are many TA patterns such as Bollinger Bands and MACD. The patterns are based on the stock prices and many times they prove to be correct predictions especially on stocks with high volume and high market caps. Patterns have been repeating themselves many times as they are driven by investors.

Sites for TA

There are many free sites for charts with explanations of their technical indicators. Popular ones include BigCharts.com, SmallCharts.com and Yahoo!Finance. Fidelity includes some unique features in its charts such as P/E.

Why I do not use TA as a primary tool for stock picking

My investing style is different from a day trader's. I prefer to 'Buy Low and Sell High' instead of 'Buy High and Sell Higher'. I try to find the real bottom price. TA will not find the bottom very easily but it tracks the trend better. As a bargain hunter, I do not expect the stock will rise fast as I'm usually swimming against the tide. However, value stocks could stay in the low price for a long time (i.e. value trap). I like to select stocks that turn around as evidenced by the SMA-20 and SMA-50.

With that said, my momentum portfolio has appreciated consistently and usually has the best performing stocks among all my portfolios. It is based on the timely grade from my subscriptions plus the metrics on timing.

Most chartists would also tell you to buy the stocks that have broken out (i.e. higher than the resistance line) and/or stocks at their highs. Contrary to value investing, you should exit when the trend reverses. The reversal could happen very fast and hence protect your portfolio by setting up stop loss (preferably with trailing stop) orders.

My opinion

I do not want to argue whether TA is good for you or not. You need to find that out. Most likely, the day traders and very short-term traders will profit more from TA than the investors seeking value stocks for the long-term gains.

Random remarks

Even if you do not use technical analysis, you should spend some time in learning it. It is better to marry fundamentals and TA. My random remarks are:

- The Institutional investors (insurance companies, pension funds, mutual funds, etc.) use TA and they MOVE the market. A lot of times it becomes a self-fulfilling prophecy. It is better to join them as most of us cannot beat them.

- Day traders take advantage of the institutional investors by spotting their trends.

- Most TA stocks should be good sized and have large average daily volumes. I prefer to use TA on value stocks to prevent long-term losses.

- I do know some folks making big money using TA, but I know more making good money using fundamentals. Since TA predicts the market better in the shorter term, its practitioners may have to pay higher taxes (in today's tax laws) in taxable accounts.

- Our objective should be making money with the least risk. Once you claim to belong to a certain group of either Fundamental or TA, you will be biased and forget your primary objective in investing.

- TA tracks the last two big market plunges (2000 and 2007) pretty well. The chart will not warn you right away for the upcoming plunge (as it depends on past data) to avoid the initial losses, but they will warn you to avoid bigger losses.

Afterthoughts

- Besides searching for stocks that have potential breakouts, we should check the stocks we owned for potential breakdowns.
  Technical Analysis tutorial.
  https://www.YouTube.com/watch?v=GENBVwV8PMs

  SMA tutorial.
  https://www.YouTube.com/watch?v=Na-ctpPsnks

Links

Fidelity video: Technical Analysis
https://www.fidelity.com/learning-center/technical-analysis/chart-types-video

Epilogue

After my early retirement, I have been spending most of my time in investing, running thousands of simulation and reading over one hundred books in investing. Starting from 2000, I have been doing extraordinary good. I comment in financial blogs and save the good ones in my own blog, so I can refer them later on. After several years, I have enough information to write a book.

At first, I want to write a book for one reader only: Me. My children have better things to do than investing. I do not need to keep my 'secrets' for them. That's why I publish this book. From the version before its release, it had been doing better than my expectation. It has been very rewarding, when my readers tell me how much they enjoy and benefit from this book.

I do not believe that this book or any book is the Holy Grail in investing. However, it has a lot of fresh ideas and good pointers that have brought me financial success (at least so far). I ask my readers to challenge my pointers and ensure they are applicable in today's market and meet their objectives and requirements.

A good pointer can make you thousands of dollars, and a bad or misinterpreted one can do the opposite. Always do paper trading on any strategy and / or idea before you commit real money on it. Start your strategy with cash in small increments until you have more confidence.

Very seldom you want to buy another book from the same author. That's why I copied many chapters from Debunk the Myths in Investing to this book.

If you believe this book is beneficial, please comment in Amazon.com or similar sites and imagine how "Complete the art of investment (Kindle version has about 850 of 6*9 pages)" would benefit you financially.

A link is provided for future updates and announcements.
https://ebmyth.blogspot.com/2020/01/updates.html

My blog: https://tonyp4idea.blogspot.com/

Appendix 1 - All my books

Book	No. of Pages	Link	ebook	Rating /5
Art of investing 5th Edition	590	Click here	link	4.5
Sector Rotation: 21 strategies 5th Edition	500	Click here	Link	9.5/10
Be a stock expert in 5 minutes. Expanded Edition.	203	Click here	Link	
Using Finviz 5th Edition	600	Click here	Link	4.5
Using Fidelity 5th Edition	600	Click here	Link	4.5
Momentum Investing 3rd Edition	285	Click here	Link	
Using profitable investing sites	520	Click here	link	
Investing successes and plunders	410	Click here	Link	
Best stocks to buy for 2025	375	Click here	Link	
Profit from bull, bear and sideway market	240	See ebook	Link	4
Artificial intelligence investing	420	See ebook	Link	
Profitable covered call	615		Link	4
Your best dollar for smart investing. $1 all the time.	65		Link	4

The ratings are usually done by ChatGPT and/or DeepSeek (AI) which

the most unbiased.

If you already have my book that is over 400 pages, most likely you do not need to buy the above books except "Investing successes and plunders" and the "Best Stock" series, which may be available every December with the title such as "Best stocks for 2026" – not a promise.

For paper-bag readers, access the links via the following link.
https://www.blogger.com/blog/post/edit/7608574268453692676/1786802320953936467

Full AI reviews on my books and articles: TonyP4Idea: Summary of AI reviews on my work

Most books have paperbacks. Links and offers are subject to change without notice. If most of your investing are in momentum/sector rotation, select "Sector Rotation 5th Edition". If not, select one from "Art of Investing 5th Edition", "Using Fidelity 5th Edition" and "Using Finviz 5th *Editon*"

*** AI Reviews:

Many thanks to the most unbiased reviews by AI. I received 4/5 stars for most of my books – it could be the highest AI would give besides the classics. Unless otherwise specified, most reviews were done in Feb., 2025. For the full review, click on the above link for the specific book.

Sector Rotation 5th Edition

Rating: 9.5/10

Sector Rotation: 5th Edition is arguably **the most complete book on sector rotation** currently available. It combines depth, practicality, and personal insight in a way that's both approachable and actionable. If you're serious about learning sector rotation or upgrading your investing strategy, this book should be on your desk—not your shelf.

Art of Investing 5th Edition

½ (4.5/5)

Art of Investing: 5th Edition is a **must-read** for investors who want to actively manage their portfolios and seek strategies beyond passive investing. Tony Pow presents a well-researched, experience-backed guide that can help investors navigate market cycles and maximize returns. If you are looking for an investing book that combines data, strategy, and personal insights, this one is worth adding to your library.

Sector Rotation 5th Edition, one of my top sellers. Your book is an impressive and valuable resource for investors interested in sector rotation. It stands out for its depth, practical strategies, and real-world examples.

🔲 **Rating: 9.5/10**
Sector Rotation: 5th Edition is arguably **the most complete book on sector rotation** currently available. It combines depth, practicality, and personal insight in a way that's both approachable and actionable. If you're serious about learning sector rotation or upgrading your investing strategy, this book should be on your desk—not your shelf.

Using Finviz 5th Edition, one of my best sellers. *Using Finviz 5th Edition* is a valuable resource for investors seeking to leverage Finviz.com effectively. Its blend of foundational principles, advanced strategies, and modern tools like AI makes it versatile. However, readers should critically assess self-reported success and adapt strategies to current market conditions. The book's reference-style format encourages revisiting chapters as skills evolve.

Recommendation:
Ideal for retail investors with basic market knowledge aiming to deepen their technical and strategic expertise. Pair with real-time market data and independent research for best results.
Rating: ★★★★☆ (4/5)
A thorough, practical guide with minor caveats around self-promotion and data timeliness

Using Fidelity 5th Edition

★★★★½ (4.5/5)

Using Fidelity: 5th Edition is an excellent guide for Fidelity customers looking to leverage the platform's research tools and advanced features. It provides in-depth investment strategies that have historically outperformed the market. While the book may feel dense at times, its wealth of knowledge makes it a highly valuable resource for serious investors. If you're looking to enhance your investing skills using Fidelity's platform, this book is a must-read.

Investing Lessons: successes and plunders

Offers a comprehensive and insightful look into investing strategies, experiences,

Best Stocks to Buy for 2025 is an excellent resource for investors seeking **data-driven, well-researched stock recommendations**. Your **historical performance, emphasis on market timing, and risk management strategies** set it apart. However, **a more structured format, better visuals, and slight content trimming** would improve readability and engagement.
and lessons learned over the years.

Profit from Bull, Bear, and Sideway Markets

It is a valuable resource for traders seeking a versatile toolkit. Its structured advice on adapting to market shifts, coupled with robust risk management frameworks, makes it a worthwhile read. While not without minor flaws—particularly in depth and modernity—it succeeds in delivering actionable insights across market cycles. Recommended for intermediate traders aiming to build resilience in volatile environments.
Rating: 4/5 (Balanced coverage and practicality offset by occasional superficiality and dated content in older editions).

Profitable Covered calls
Overall Rating:
☆ ☆ ☆ ☆ (4/5) – A valuable resource for covered call strategies, especially for investors who want a mix of personal experience and market insights. With better editing and organization, it could be a top-tier investing guide.

Shorting stocks and ETFs
Final Verdict:
Your book is an excellent resource for intermediate to advanced investors looking to deepen their knowledge of short selling and market timing. With some refinements in structure and editing, it could be even more impactful. Rated at 4/5.

Artificial Intelligence Investing. Tony Pow's book, *Artificial Intelligence Investing*, is a detailed guide for investors looking to capitalize on the AI revolution. It combines practical investment strategies with insights into the future of AI and its impact on various sectors. The author's emphasis on risk management, market timing, and long-term value investing makes this book a valuable resource for both novice and seasoned investors.

Profitable Covered Call. Overall Rating:
☆ ☆ ☆ ☆ (4/5) – A valuable resource for covered call strategies, especially for investors who want a mix of personal experience and market insights. With better editing and organization, it could be a top-tier investing guide.

Best stocks to buy for 2025

The current book is "Best stocks for 2025" in this series.
https://www.amazon.com/dp/B0D2459JDT
If available, future books could be titled "for 2026" around Dec. 20, 2025).
If the sales of my books in this series were based on past performances, I should have sold many books, but obviously not.

Book	Stocks	Return[3]	Ann.	Beat RSP by[1]
Best stocks to buy for 2024	8	46%	48%	132%
Best stocks to buy for 2023	8	36%	36%	290%
Best stocks to buy for 2022	10[6]	4%	4%	153%[7]
Best Stocks to buy as of July, 2021[4]	8	5%	13%	487%
Best Stocks for 2021 2nd Edition	10	42%[4]	52%	220%
Best Stocks for 2021	4	29%	44%	118%
Best Stocks to Buy from Aug, 2020	14	45%	45%	3%[5]
Avg.	9	34%	40%	208%[2]

Here is the detail:
https://tonyp4idea.blogspot.com/2024/12/best-stocks-to-buy-for-2025.html

Art of Investing

Art of Investing 5th Edition consisting of 15 books in 1. Besides saving money and your digital shelve space, it gives you quick reference and concentration on the topic you're currently interested in. It covers most investing topics in investing excluding speculative investing such as currency trading and day trading. It has over 600 pages (6*9), about the size of two investing books of average size. If you have any of my investing books less than 200 pages, this is the one for your **next reading.**

The 15 books

Book No.	Amazon.com
1	Simple techniques
2	Finding Stocks
3	Evaluating Stocks
4	Scoring Stocks
5	Trading Stocks
6	Market Timing
7	Strategies
8	Sector Rotation
9	Insider Trading
10	Penny Stocks & Micro Cap
11	Momentum Investing
12	Dividend Investing
13	Technical Analysis
14	Investing Ideas
15	Buffettology

The book links are subject to change without notice.

"How to be a billionaire" is for beginners and couch potatoes, who can use the advanced features of this book in the simplest and less time-consuming techniques. Most advance users can skip this section unless they want to use some of the short cuts described.

We start with the basic books Finding Stocks, Evaluate Stocks, Trading Stocks and Market Timing. You can select and start with one of the many styles and strategies in investing such as swing trading and top-down strategy. Many tools are described in other books such as ETFs, technical analysis, covered calls and trading plan.

Many books start with "Why" to lure you to read more and are followed by "How" and then the theory behind the book.
If the book you're reading is beneficial to you, imagine how it would with 850 pages.

\# Most readers' comments are on "Debunk the Myths in Investing", which this book is originally based on. As of 2018, I did not know any of the commentators on my books.

"I skipped ahead to his chapter book 14 (of "Complete the Art of Investing"), Investment Advice just to get a feel of his writing style. His research is phenomenal and doesn't overwhelm with big words or catchy "sales-like" tactics.

I truly believe this ordinary man, Mr. Tony Pow, has a gift of explaining his experience as an investor without the bull crap of trying to make you buy his stuff. He seemingly just wants to share his knowledge, tips, and clarity of definitions for the kind of folks like me who want to understand something FIRST before jumping in with emotions of trying to make a boat load of money. I like the technical analysis side he brings.

Mr. Tony Pow talks about hidden gems in his book; well....quite frankly, he is a hidden gem. Thank you and I will also post my comments about this author to my Facebook page!" – JB on this book.

"Excellent book, recommend to all investors... great knowledge. It has fine-tuned my investing strategies... Your book is hard to set aside, as I read it all the time learning good techniques and analysis of stocks, ETF... Since I purchased your book in March, I have underlined, highlighted and placed tabs on top of pages for quick reference." – Aileron on this book.

"Tony, I just finished reading your 2nd edition. It's my pleasure to report that I found it most interesting. You're welcome to use this blurb if you like:

Debunk the Myths in Investing is an all-encompassing look at not only the most salient factors influencing markets and investors, but also a from-the-trenches look at many of the misconceptions and mistakes too many investors make. Reading this book may save not only time and aggravation but money as well!"

Joseph Shaefer, CEO, Stanford Wealth Management LLC.

"Tony, Great work!" from James and Chris, who are portfolio managers.

"'Debunk the Myths in Investing' is a comprehensive book on investing that deals with many aspects of this tense profession in which with a lot of knowledge and a bit of luck (or vice versa) one can greatly benefit...

Therefore 'Debunk the Myths in Investing' is an interesting book that on its 500 pages offer a lot of knowledge related to investing world and many practical advice, so I can recommend its reading if you're interested in this topic."
- Denis Vukosav, Top 500 Reviewers at Amazon.com.

"490 pages (Debunk) of a genius's ranting and hypothesis with various theories throughout, written light-heartedly with ample doses of humor...Yes, the myth of not being able to profitably time the market is BUSTED...

One might ask... Why is he giving away the results of his hard-earned research for only $20? He states that his children are not interested in investing and wants to share his efforts with the world." - Abe Agoda.

"Excellent book, recommend to all investors... great knowledge. It has fine-tuned my investing strategies... Your book is hard to set aside, as I read it all the time learning good techniques and analysis of stocks, ETF... Since I purchased your book in March, I have underlined, highlighted and placed tabs on top of pages for quick reference." - Aileron on this book.

"Great stuff, Tony. It's great to meet experienced traders such as yourself. I had a browse through the book and think your method is a little more refined than mine."
"Your strategy is very rules based and solid. I sometimes envy people who have developed something like this."

Making 50% in one month
I claim to have the best one-month performance ever for recommending 8 or more stocks without using options and leverage. My following return is 57% in a month or 621% annualized. They are slightly different as I calculated the average from the averages of three different accounts. The average buy date is 12/26/18 and the "current date" is 01/28/19.

The performance may not be repeated. I will use the same screen for the coming years and even the expected 10% (or 120% annualized) is very good.

I used the same screen for searching stock candidates. I spent a total of about 20 hours from Dec. 15, 2018 to Jan. 5, 2019.

Stock	Buy Price	Sold or Current Price	Buy date	Sold or Current date	Profit %	Profit % Ann.	Status
CHK	2.13	2.99	01/03/09	01/18/19	40%	982%	Sold
MNK	16.41	21.45	01/03/19	01/25/19	31%	510%	Sold
MNK	16.43	21.45	01/03/19	01/25/19	31%	507%	Sold
NNBR	5.68	8.58	12/26/18	01/28/19	51%	565%	
NNBR	5.72	8.58	12/26/18	01/28/19	66%	727%	
ESTE	4.35	6.45	12/26/18	01/18/19	48%	766%	Sold
LCI	4.61	8.29	12/21/18	01/28/19	80%	767%	
MDR	8.01	9.13	01/08/19	01/28/19	14%	255%	
YRCW	3.29	5.78	12/21/18	01/28/19	76%	727%	
YRCW	3.26	5.78	12/21/18	01/28/19	77%	742%	
ASRT	3.56	4.18	12/26/18	01/28/19	17%	193%	
UTCC	7.13	11.00	12/26/18	01/28/19	54%	600%	
YRCW	2.92	5.78	12/26/18	01/28/19	98%	1083%	

Best one-year return

I claim to have the best-performed article in Seeking Alpha history, an investing site, for recommending 15 or more stocks in one year after the publish date without using options and leverage.

https://seekingalpha.com/article/1095671-amazing-returns-velti-alcatel-lucent-alpha-natural-resources

Appendix 2: Reviews by the unbiased AI

Many thanks to the most unbiased reviews by AI. My following books were rated from 8 to 9.5 out of 10. Recently, DeepSeek does not review books over a specific size.

I accept all suggestions. However, I did repeat a few important concepts, so the reader does not have to waste time in searching for them. Some examples are older for a good reason. For example, if I did not use the market crash of 2000, I only had one market crash to illustrate. It is always better to follow the winners, though I have included my blunders in investing.

Review of "Art of Investing 5th Edition " 9/10

ChatGPT Review

Overall Impression:
Art of Investing: 5th Edition is an extensive, well-structured guide designed for investors of all levels. With over 600 pages, it offers a deep dive into investing strategies, market timing, risk management, and stock selection. The book blends personal experience with data-driven techniques, making it both informative and practical.

Strengths:

- ✅ **Comprehensive Coverage** – The book spans 16 "mini-books," covering everything from beginner investing techniques to advanced stock scoring, market cycles, and sector rotation strategies. It even includes guidance on artificial intelligence in investing.
- ✅ **Proven Strategies** – The author shares his own investment successes, highlighting methods that have consistently outperformed the S&P 500. His use of sector rotation, fundamental analysis, and market timing offers valuable insights.
- ✅ **Practicality & Accessibility** – The book is structured as a reference manual rather than a linear read, allowing investors to jump to relevant sections. It also includes actionable advice, checklists, and step-by-step guides.
- ✅ **Personal Insights & Humor** – The inclusion of personal anecdotes, humor, and lighthearted "fillers" makes the book more engaging than a traditional investing manual.
- ✅ **Use of Free Tools** – The book extensively references resources like Finviz, Fidelity, and ETFdb, making sophisticated analysis accessible to retail investors without costly subscriptions.

Areas for Improvement:

- ♦ **Length & Density** – At over 600 pages, the book is packed with information, which can be overwhelming for beginners. A more concise version or a summary section for each chapter could improve readability.

- **Editing & Formatting** – Some sections could benefit from tighter editing to improve flow and readability. The humor and filler content, while entertaining, might feel excessive for readers looking for a purely analytical approach.
- **Market Timing Debate** – While the book provides strong evidence supporting market timing strategies, some traditional investors may find this approach debatable, as it contradicts the "buy and hold" philosophy endorsed by many long-term investors.

Final Verdict:

★ ★ ★ ★ ½ (4.5/5)

Art of Investing: 5th Edition is a must-read for investors who want to actively manage their portfolios and seek strategies beyond passive investing. Tony Pow presents a well-researched, experience-backed guide that can help investors navigate market cycles and maximize returns. If you are looking for an investing book that combines data, strategy, and personal insights, this one is worth adding to your library.

DeepSeek Review

Your book, *Art of Investing 5th Edition*, is a comprehensive and practical guide that caters to investors of all levels, from beginners to advanced fund managers. Here's a review based on the content provided:

Strengths:

1. **Comprehensive Coverage:**
    - The book covers a wide range of topics, from basic investment strategies to advanced techniques like sector rotation, market timing, and insider trading. It's structured into 16 interconnected "books," each focusing on specific aspects of investing, making it both a reference guide and a practical manual.
2. **Proven Strategies:**
    - You share your personal investment strategies and techniques, many of which have been proven to outperform the market. For example, your sector rotation strategy has yielded returns exceeding five times your initial investment, and your stock recommendations have consistently beaten the S&P 500.
3. **Practical Tools and Resources:**
    - The book emphasizes the use of free or low-cost tools like Finviz, Fidelity, and ETFdb, making it accessible to retail investors. You also provide step-by-step instructions on how to use these tools effectively.
4. **Risk Management:**
    - You stress the importance of risk management, advocating for stop-loss orders, diversification, and avoiding leverage for beginners. This is crucial for long-term success in investing.

5. **Market Timing:**
   - Your market timing techniques, particularly the use of SMA (Simple Moving Averages) and RSI (Relative Strength Index), are well-explained and have been effective in avoiding major market downturns.
6. **Personal Insights:**
   - You share your personal successes and mistakes, making the content relatable and actionable. This transparency adds credibility and helps readers learn from your experiences.
7. **Focus on Education:**
   - The book encourages readers to practice with paper trading and provides practical exercises. This hands-on approach is beneficial for beginners who need to build confidence before investing real money.
8. **AI Integration:**
   - The inclusion of AI tools like ChatGPT and DeepSeek for stock analysis and market predictions is forward-thinking, though you caution readers about the limitations of outdated databases.

Weaknesses:
1. **Dense and Lengthy:**
   - While the book is comprehensive, its length (770 pages) and density might be overwhelming for some readers, especially beginners. The sheer volume of information could make it difficult to digest in one go.
2. **Outdated Data:**
   - Some of the examples and data, particularly those related to specific stocks or market conditions, may become outdated quickly. While you advise readers to focus on the rationale behind the examples rather than the specific stocks, this could still be a limitation.
3. **Complexity for Beginners:**
   - Although you provide beginner-friendly sections, some of the advanced techniques (e.g., short selling, momentum investing) might still be too complex for novice investors. The book could benefit from more simplified explanations or additional beginner-focused content.
4. **Over-Reliance on Specific Tools:**
   - The book heavily relies on specific tools like Finviz and Fidelity. While these are excellent resources, readers who prefer other platforms might find it challenging to adapt the strategies to their preferred tools.
5. **AI Limitations:**
   - While the integration of AI is innovative, the reliance on AI tools like ChatGPT and DeepSeek comes with the caveat that their databases may not be up-to-date. This could lead to

outdated or inaccurate recommendations, which you acknowledge but could be a concern for readers.

Overall Impression:
Art of Investing 5th Edition is a valuable resource for anyone looking to improve their investment skills. It's particularly well-suited for intermediate to advanced investors who are familiar with the basics and are looking to refine their strategies. The book's strength lies in its practical, actionable advice and the author's willingness to share personal insights and proven techniques.

However, beginners might find the book overwhelming due to its length and the complexity of some topics. Additionally, while the inclusion of AI tools is innovative, readers should be cautious about relying too heavily on them due to potential data limitations.

Final Verdict:
Overall, *Art of Investing 5th Edition* is a solid, well-researched, and practical guide that offers a wealth of information for investors. It's a must-read for those who are serious about improving their investment acumen and achieving long-term financial success. However, beginners may need to take it slow and focus on the foundational sections before diving into the more advanced strategies.
Rating: 4.5/5

"Using Finviz 5th Editon" and "Using Fidelity 5th Edition" are similar to "Art of Investing" with changes specific to the topic.

"Using Finviz" is rated 8/10: TonyP4Idea: Review of "Using Finviz 5th Edition"

"Using Fidelity is rated 9/10: TonyP4Idea: Review of "Using Fidelity 5th Edition"

Review of " Best stocks to buy for 2025"

Your book, **Best Stocks to Buy for 2025 (Note:** *the next book is "2026")*, is a highly detailed and data-driven investment guide that builds on the success of previous editions. Here's a structured review of its strengths and areas for improvement.

Strengths:
1. Proven Track Record
- You provide historical performance data from previous editions, showing that your stock picks have consistently outperformed the RSP (equal-weight S&P 500 ETF).
- The book highlights an average outperformance of over 200% across past editions, reinforcing credibility.

2. Comprehensive Stock Selection Strategy
- The book includes a **Primary List** for long-term investing and multiple **sub-lists** for short-term trading (3-month and 6-month holding periods).
- Uses fundamental metrics, Finviz screening, and AI-generated stock ideas for diverse stock selection.

3. Practical Investing Insights
- Explores short-term and long-term strategies, including momentum trades and market timing approaches.
- Discusses stop-loss techniques, trailing stops, and how to protect profits effectively.

4. Market Timing & Risk Management
- Includes detailed insights on market cycles, bear market indicators, and strategies to hedge against downturns.
- The book's emphasis on **when** to invest (market timing) rather than just **what** to buy adds significant value.

5. Educational Value
- Goes beyond stock recommendations by covering fundamental analysis, technical indicators (Bollinger Bands, RSI, MACD), and investment psychology.
- Offers a structured approach, making it suitable for both beginners and seasoned investors.

Areas for Improvement:
1. Organization & Readability
- The book is **very dense** (over 375 pages), which can be overwhelming.
- Consider **streamlining the layout** by adding bullet points, clearer section breaks, and summaries at the end of each chapter.

2. More Visual Aids
- While data tables are helpful, adding **more charts, graphs, and stock performance visuals** would make complex ideas easier to grasp.

3. Conciseness

- Some sections, particularly on past performance, are **repetitive**.
- Shortening these parts or summarizing key findings in a table format could improve readability.

4. More Case Studies & Examples
- Including **detailed breakdowns of past successful trades** would enhance the learning experience.
- A step-by-step example of how a selected stock performed over time, including entry and exit points, could be valuable.

Final Thoughts:
Best Stocks to Buy for 2025 is an excellent resource for investors seeking **data-driven, well-researched stock recommendations**. Your **historical performance, emphasis on market timing, and risk management strategies** set it apart.

However, **a more structured format, better visuals, and slight content trimming** would improve readability and engagement.

"I have read your book : "Stocks To Buy 2024" and it's excellent. I keep it close to me and read it sometimes to remind me some principles. It's in my top 5 and I've read more than a hundred ones." – Eric, 3/23/2025

Review of "Sector Rotation 5th Edition" rated 9.5

Overview
Tony Pow's *Sector Rotation: 5th Edition* is an exceptionally thorough and practical guide that stands out in the crowded field of investment literature. With over 500 pages and 21 distinct strategies, this book offers a deep dive into the theory and execution of sector rotation, drawing on the author's decades of hands-on experience and real-world performance.

Strengths

☑ **Unmatched Strategy Depth**
- The book covers **21 sector rotation strategies**, far surpassing competing titles that usually offer only one or two.
- It includes approaches ranging from simple ETF-and-cash rotation for beginners to advanced momentum, contrarian, insider, and macroeconomic strategies.

☑ **Proven Performance**
- Pow backs his strategies with concrete results—including a **fivefold portfolio growth** through sector rotation, and outperformance of the S&P 500 by nearly **184%** across his recent book series.
- Specific calls, like recommending SMCI with a 272% return (Tony: my first twelve bagger at its peak), and oil at the 2016 bottom, establish his credibility.

☑ **Tailored for All Investor Levels**
- The book includes dedicated sections for beginners, intermediate, and advanced investors.
- Each strategy is labeled with difficulty and practical tips, helping readers choose based on experience and time commitment.

☑ **Educational + Entertaining**
- Pow intersperses serious content with humor, real-life anecdotes, and fillers to lighten the tone—creating an educational yet engaging read.
- AI-assisted summaries and commentary from tools like ChatGPT and DeepSeek help distill complex topics into actionable insights.

☑ **Practical Tools and Real-World Application**
- Heavy use of **Finviz, Fidelity, and ETF databases** for real-time sector evaluation.
- Uses technical indicators like RSI(14), SMA, MACD in a digestible, non-overwhelming way.
- Includes links to video tutorials and online references to support readers using digital versions.

Areas for Improvement

⚠ **Length and Redundancy**

- At over 500 pages, the book can be overwhelming. While repetition helps reinforce concepts, some ideas are restated more often than necessary.

Flow and Navigation
- The structure is more reference-like than linear. Beginners might benefit from a "quick-start roadmap" or flowchart to guide initial reading.

Design and Formatting
- Some visual elements (e.g., charts and tables) may not render well on small e-reader screens. The author does note this and offers workarounds.

Noteworthy Features
- **AI Integration:** The book leverages ChatGPT and DeepSeek to review, polish, and even write several sections—showcasing how investors can benefit from AI in content creation and market analysis.
- **Humility and Honesty:** The author shares not only successes but also missed opportunities and mistakes, offering readers real insight into risk management and psychological pitfalls.
- **Top-Down & Bottom-Up Coverage:** The mix of macroeconomic cycle theories (e.g., sector sensitivity to interest rates and politics) with micro-level stock selection tools makes this comprehensive.

Final Verdict

Rating: 9.5/10

Sector Rotation: 5th Edition is arguably **the most complete book on sector rotation** currently available. It combines depth, practicality, and personal insight in a way that's both approachable and actionable. If you're serious about learning sector rotation or upgrading your investing strategy, this book should be on your desk—not your shelf.

Review of "Your first dollar for smart investing "

ChatGPT

✅ Strengths

1. Clear Purpose and Audience

- The book clearly targets beginners and delivers on that goal.
- Your tone is friendly, practical, and non-patronizing — perfect for newcomers.
- It positions the "first dollar" wisely — focusing on security, simplicity, and learning.

2. Actionable Advice

- You emphasize using ETFs like VOO/SPY, avoiding leverage, setting stop losses, and using practical tools like Finviz, which are great entry-level practices.
- The step-by-step guidance for evaluating stocks, ETF analysis, and market timing is simplified but effective.
- Including your personal recommendations, tools, and specific links (e.g., YouTube, Fidelity, Finviz) gives readers clear next steps.

3. Unique Selling Points

- Priced at $1, it truly aligns with the concept: smart investing starts with smart spending.
- The integration of AI (like ChatGPT and DeepSeek) as co-editors and advisors is forward-looking and distinguishes this from traditional investing books.

- Many sections feel like a hybrid of personal coaching and DIY investing — a rare tone in finance books.

❈ Final Thoughts

This book is well-aligned for its purpose and price:

- **Approachable, practical, and authentic.**
- A **useful primer** that competes well with free articles or $20+ beginner guides.

Final Thoughts from DeepSeek:

Tony Pow's book delivers on its promise: a **budget-friendly, no-nonsense guide** for investing newcomers. Its strengths lie in simplicity and actionable steps, though it lacks depth for seasoned readers. The AI-assisted content is a novelty, but the real value is in the foundational advice—perfect for someone investing their "first dollar."

Rating: ★★★★☆ (4/5)
Recommendation: Highly

Reviewd on 5/28/2025

Review of "Momentum Investing 3rd Edition "

Strengths:
1. **Extensive Data & Performance Tracking** – You provide a thorough history of your momentum stock trades, including real-world examples and performance analysis, which adds credibility.
2. **Diverse Momentum Strategies** – You break momentum investing into multiple strategies, catering to different holding periods and risk tolerances.
3. **Sector Rotation & Market Timing** – The book successfully integrates sector rotation and market timing to enhance momentum strategies.
4. **Practical Implementation** – Step-by-step guides on using platforms like Finviz, Seeking Alpha, and Fidelity make it easy for readers to apply the strategies.
5. **Personal Investment Experience** – Your personal trading history and transparent performance records provide valuable lessons for readers.

Final Verdict:
This is an in-depth and practical guide for momentum investors, backed by real-world experience.

Review of "Using profitable investment sites" rated 8

Strengths
- **Comprehensive Coverage** – The book provides in-depth discussions on various investment platforms, strategies, and techniques, covering fundamental and technical analysis, sector rotation, market timing, and more.
- **Practical Insights** – You include personal investment experiences and strategies, making the content relatable and actionable for readers.
- **Structured for Different Investors** – It caters to beginner, intermediate, and advanced investors, helping readers navigate content at their level.
- **Focus on Market Timing & Sector Rotation** – These strategies can be useful for those looking to enhance returns beyond standard buy-and-hold approaches.
- **Use of Free and Paid Investment Tools** – The book effectively highlights how to leverage platforms like Barron's, Finviz, and Seeking Alpha for research.

Final Verdict
- **Rating: 4/5**

Your book is a **valuable resource for self-directed investors**, particularly those interested in using online tools for research and market timing. With tighter editing and better visual organization, it could become an even more **impactful investment guide**.

Review of "Investing successes and blunders"

Strengths:
1. **Practical Experience:** Your personal investing experiences, both successes and mistakes, add authenticity and credibility. Readers can learn from real-life examples rather than just theoretical concepts.
2. **Data-Driven Approach:** Your detailed performance tracking of stock picks and strategies over multiple years demonstrates a commitment to rigorous analysis.
3. **Market Timing Insights:** The emphasis on simple market timing techniques and avoiding common pitfalls, such as emotional investing and overreliance on government policies, is valuable.
4. **Sector-Specific Insights:** Your discussion of various market sectors, including AI, real estate, bonds, and commodities, helps readers understand different investment opportunities.

Risk Management: Your explanations of calculated vs. blind risks, the importance of diversification, and strategies like stop-loss orders are useful for investors at all levels.

Appendix 3 - Our window to the investing world

The paperback version of this chapter can be found in the following link.
http://ebmyth.blogspot.com/2013/11/web-sites.html

- **General**
  Wikipedia / Investopedia /Yahoo!Finance / MarketWatch / Cnnfn / Morningstar /CNBC / Bloomberg / WSJ / Barron's / Motley Fool / TheStreet
- **Evaluate stocks**
  Finviz / SeekingAlpha / MSN Money / Zacks / Daily Finance / ADR / Fidelity / Earnings Impact / OpenInsider / NYSE / NASDAQ / SEC / SEC for 10K and 10Q (quarterly) reports required to file for listed stocks in major exchanges.
- **Charts**
  BigCharts / FreeStockCharts / StockCharts /
- **Screens**
  Yahoo!Finance / Finviz / CNBC / Morningstar /
- **Besides stocks**
  123Jump / Hoover's Online / FINRA Bond Market Data / REIT / Commodity Futures / Option Industry
- **Vendors**
  AAII / Zacks / IBD / GuruFocus / VectorVest / Fidelity / Interactive Brokers / Merrill Lynch /
- **Economy.**
  Econday / EcoconStats / Federal Reserve / Economist /
- **Misc.**
  Dow Jones Indices / Russell / Wilshire / IRS / Wikinvest / ETF Database / ETF Trends / Nolo (estate planning) / AARP /

Appendix 4 - ETFs / Mutual Funds

What is an ETF
ETFs have basic differences from mutual funds: 1. Lower management expenses, 2. Trade ETFs same as stocks, and 3. Usually more diversified but not more selective than the related mutual funds such as NOBL vs FRDPX.

The major classifications of ETFs are 1. Simulating an index such as SPY, QQQ and DIA, 2. Simulating a sector such as XLE and SOXX, 3. Simulating an asset class such as GLD and SLV, 4. Simulating a country or a group of countries such as EWC and FXI, 5. Managed by a manager(s) such as ARKK, 6. Betting a market or sector to go down such as SH and PSQ, and 7. Leveraged (not recommended for beginners).
Fidelity: Index ETFs (https://www.fidelity.com/etfs/overview).
Wikipedia on ETF (http://en.wikipedia.org/wiki/Exchange-traded_fund).

List of ETFs
ETF database (Recommended): http://etfdb.com/
ETF Bloomberg: http://www.bloomberg.com/markets/etfs/
ETF Trends: http://www.etftrends.com/
A list of ETFs. Seeking Alpha.
http://etf.stock-encyclopedia.com/category/)
A list of contra ETFs (or bear ETFs)
http://www.tradermike.net/inverse-short-etfs-bearish-ctf-funds/
Misc.: ETFGuide, ETFReplay
Fidelity low-cost index funds:
https://www.youtube.com/watch?v=zpKi4_IJvlY
Fidelity Annuity funds with performance data.
http://fundresearch.fidelity.com/annuities/category-performance-annual-total-returns-quarterly/FPRAI?refann=005
ETFs vs mutual funds; https://www.youtube.com/watch?v=Vmz0CzlQvHk
Three ETFs: https://www.youtube.com/watch?v=MVi2RhpffuU

Other resources
Most subscription services offer research on ETFs. IBD has a strategy dedicated to ETFs and so does AAII to name a couple. Seeking Alpha has extensive resources for ETF including an ETF screener and investing ideas. So is ETFdb.

Not all ETFs are created equal
Check their performances and their expenses.

When to use or not to use ETFs
I prefer sector mutual funds in some industries, as they have many bad stocks such as drug industry, banks, miners and insurers. Most mutual funds cannot time the market.

When you believe a sector is heading up (or contra ETF for heading down), but you do not have time to do research on specific stocks, buy an ETF for the sector; it is same for the market.

Half ETF
Taking out half of the stocks that score below the average in an index ETF could beat the same full ETF itself. I call it HETF (half the ETF). You heard it here first. After a decade, at least one company has a similar product.

To illustrate, sort the expected P/E (not including stocks with negative earnings) in ascending order and only include the stocks on the first half. Add more fundamental metrics. It will take a few minutes.

Disadvantages of ETFs
- When you have two stocks in a sector ETF one good one and one bad one, the ETF treats them the same. Stock pickers would buy the one that has a better appreciation potential.
- Sometimes the return could be misleading due to stock rotation. To illustrate this, on August 29, 2012, SHLD was replaced by LYB in a sector fund. SHLD was down by 4% and LYB was up by 4% primarily due to the switch. Unless you sell and buy at the right time (which is impossible), your return would not match the ETF's returns due to the replacement.
- Ensure the performance matches the corresponding index; it is hard due to excluding dividends.

Advantages of ETFs
- We have demonstrated that you can beat the market by using market timing. Between 2000 and Nov., 2013, you only exit and reenter the market 3 times and the result is astonishing.
- It is easy to rotate a sector vs. buying/selling all of the stocks in this sector. Rotating a sector is the same as trading a stock.
- The risk is spread out, and your portfolio is diversified especially for a market ETF or buying three or more ETFs in different sectors.
- Periodically the bad stocks in most funds are replaced by better stocks.
- Eliminate the time in researching stocks.

Leveraged ETFs
I do not recommend them. Some are 2x, 3x and even higher. They're too risky for beginners. However, when you are very sure or your tested

strategy has very low drawdown, you may want to use them to improve performance. Most leveraged ETFs and contra ETFs have higher fees.

My basic ETF tables
I include some contra ETFs, mutual funds and Fidelity's annuity. Some of these may be interesting to you. Most Vanguard's ETFs have lower fees.

ETFs and funds come and go. Some ideas and classifications are my own interpretation. Refer to ETFdb for updated information. Not responsible for any error. Check out the ETF or fund before you take any action.

I prefer VFINX over SPY for the lower fees; both simulate the S&P 500 index. The stocks in the ETF can be either equally weighted or weighted by market caps. The latter is more like using momentum strategy, as the rising stocks usually have larger market caps. The index usually kicks out some poor-performing stocks and replaced them with better stocks. These ETFs are suited for long-term investing without constant reviews.

Table by market cap:

Category	ETF	Mutual Funds	Fidelity's Annuity	Contra ETF	Alternate
Size:					
Large Cap	DIA			DOG	
	SPY			SH	VOO VFINX RSP FXAIX
	QQQ			PSQ	FNCMX
	RYH				
Blend	IWD	BEQGX			
Growth	SPYG	FBGRX			FSPGX
Value	SPYV	DOGGX			FLCOX
Dividend	NOBL	FRDPX			
	VYM				
Mid Cap			FNBSC	MYY	
Blend	MDY	VSEQX			
Growth		STDIX			
		BPTRX			
Value		FSMVX			
Small Cap			FPRGC	SBB	FSSNX
Blend	IWM	HDPSX			
Growth		PRDSX			FECGX
Value		SKSEX			FISVX
Micro	IWC				

Multi				
Blend		VDEOX		
Growth		VHCOX		
Value		TCLCX		
Total				FSKAX VTI
Bond				
Long Term (20)	VLV	BTTTX	TBF	
Mid Term (7 – 10)	VCIT	FSTGX		
Short Term (1 – 3 yrs.)	VCSH	THOPX		
Total	BOND	PONDX		
Corp Invest Grade	VCIT	NTHEX		
High Yield (junk)	PHB	SPHIX		
Muni	MUB	Check state		
Special situation				
Buy back	PKW			

Table by sectors:

Sector	ETF	Mutual Funds	Fidelity's Annuity
Banking[1]		FSRBK	
Regional	IAT		
Biotech	IBB	FBIOX	
	XBI	Large	
Consumer Dis.	XLY	FSCPX	FVHAC
Consumer Staple	XLP	FDFAX	FCSAC
Defense + Aero	PPA		
Finance	KIE	FIDSX	FONNC
	IYF		
Energy	XLE	FSENX	FJLLC
Energy Service		FSESX	
Farm	DBA		
Gold	GLD	FSAGX	BAR
Gold Miner	GDX	VGPMX	
Health Care	IYH	FSPHX	FPDRC
	VHT	VGHCX	
House Builder	ITB	FSHOX	
Industrial	IYJ	FCYIX	FBALC

Material	VAW	FSDPX	GSG
	IYM		
Natural Gas	UNG		
Oil	USO		
Oil Service	OIH	FSESX	
Oil Exploration	XOP		
Real Estate	VNQ	FRIFX	FFWLC
REIT	VNQ		
Retail	RTH	FSRPX	
	XRT		
Regional bank	KRE	FSRBX	
Semi Conduct	SMH		
Software	XSW	FSCSX	
	IGV		
Technology	XLK	FSPTX	FYENC
	FDN	FBSOX	
		ROGSX	
Telecomm.	VOX	FSTCX	FVTAC
Transport	XTN		
	IYT		
Utilities	XLU	FSUTX	FKMSC
Wireless		FWRLX	

Footnote. [1] Also check Finance.

Table by countries outside the USA:

Country	ETF	Mutual Funds	Fidelity's Annuity	Alternate
Australia	EWA			
Brazil	EWZ			
Canada	EWC	FICDX		
China	FXI	FHKCX		
EAFE	EFA			
Emerging	VWO	FEMEX	FEMAC	FPADX
Europe	VGK	FIEUX		
Global	KXI	PGVFX		
Greece	GREK			
India	INDY	MINDX		
Indonesia	EIDO			
Latin America	ILF	FLATX		
Nordic		FNORX		
Hong Kong	EWH			
Japan	EWJ	FJPNX		

S. Africa	EZA			
S. Korea	EWY	MAKOX		
Singapore	EWS			
Taiwan	EWT			
Turkey	TUR			
United Kingdom	EWU			
Foreign:				
Combination				
Intern. Div.	IDV			FTIHX
Small Cap	SCZ			
Value	EFV			
Europe	VGK			

Appendix 5 - Links

The following may be repeated from the articles and it is for your convenience. To illustrate, Under YouTube (or Investopedia), search "Finviz". Some links have permanent values such as most articles from Wikipedia and Investopedia. Others reflect current events such as the current market. Learn from them and act when the current events have similar descriptions. For the printed versions and updated links, enter the following in your browser: https://tonyp4idea.blogspot.com/2023/02/links-in-my-books.html

Beginners

Common mistakes: https://www.youtube.com/watch?v=zkNueyFs8zQ

Best Vanguard ETFs https://www.youtube.com/watch?v=mSEyghlZchQ

Buy stocks/ETFs: https://www.youtube.com/watch?v=4vjkeC_4EmU

Screener

Finviz https://www.youtube.com/watch?v=cHNUMPgEYGY

Recommended YouTube: https://www.youtube.com/watch?v=CJoN7wLfWNo
PEG: http://en.wikipedia.org/wiki/PEG_ratio
Short %:
http://www.investopedia.com/university/shortselling/shortselling1.asp#axzz2LNDvpemo
Openinsider: http://www.openinsider.com/
Finviz: http://Finviz.com/
terms: http://www.Finviz.com/help/screener.ashx
Insider Cow: http://www.insidercow.com/
Current Ratio: http://en.wikipedia.org/wiki/Current_ratio
Cash Flow: https://www.youtube.com/watch?v=1v8hRZ36--c
Balance sheet: https://www.youtube.com/watch?v=DZjU0CHKyV4
How to find quality stocks.
http://seekingalpha.com/article/2381395-how-to-identify-quality-stocks-and-is-there-really-alpha-to-be-had

Investing strategies

Inflation: https://www.youtube.com/watch?v=Zpthvpy3UKg\

Swing: https://www.youtube.com/watch?v=C9EQkA7uVU8
https://www.youtube.com/watch?v=a_wpfSXRSjo
https://www.youtube.com/watch?v=M8sNMhPJIN

Momentum: https://www.youtube.com/watch?v=PpUlOyZrl9
Penny stocks: https://www.youtube.com/watch?v=u7xZ3kF62u4

Scanning https://www.youtube.com/watch?v=7iZpWmwBhel

Peter lynch 2023: https://www.youtube.com/watch?v=CK1AkVVVXu8

Charlie: https://www.youtube.com/watch?v=8g2B6QJ2FEc
Dividend ETFs: https://www.youtube.com/watch?v=64NEiyoNBIM

- Innovative sectors: https://www.youtube.com/watch?v=Ll1hMX8qtHg

Trading stocks
Beginners: https://www.youtube.com/watch?v=aod3cyUEu4k
Covered call https://www.youtube.com/watch?v=dzMOnI4Fh04

Tax Avoidance: http://en.wikipedia.org/wiki/Tax_avoidance
Tax Law: http://en.wikipedia.org/wiki/Income_tax_%28U.S.%29
Without paying (gift tax):
http://en.wikipedia.org/wiki/Gift_tax_in_the_United_States#Gift_tax_exemptions
http://www.irs.gov/Businesses/Small-Businesses-&-Self-Employed/What%27s-New---Estate-and-Gift-Tax
AMT: http://en.wikipedia.org/wiki/Alternative_minimum_tax
Estate planning fun. http://tonyp4idea.blogspot.com/2014/08/estate-planning-101-for-me.html
Taxes on stocks: https://www.youtube.com/watch?v=EKYMbsjUUtE
Tax avoidance: https://www.youtube.com/watch?v=tXou5pM7zh0
Capital gain: https://www.youtube.com/watch?v=ezPs4ibFsNU&t=2678s
Trading course: https://www.youtube.com/watch?v=8sbfrusR5Eo
How safe our brokers. https://www.youtube.com/watch?v=wz64z1YuL0A

Fidelity funds: https://www.youtube.com/watch?v=xdEunmLrhb4
Fidelity core money market fund:
https://www.youtube.com/watch?v=KU6HYRHj3jg

Government bond default? https://www.youtube.com/watch?v=wMxj6iB92ZA
Broker CDs (Recommended): https://www.youtube.com/watch?v=zhEiyW2N7KE
Money market fund: https://www.youtube.com/watch?v=N53wZ_80abU

Economy
YouTube video (highly recommended):
https://www.youtube.com/watch?v=Q6NIDJZdQH4

What will the world be in 5 years (2027).
https://www.youtube.com/watch?v=LzipwDQBUyc

Inflation and interest rate: https://www.youtube.com/watch?v=q8KJSNyAHLE

Wealth gap widens with low interest rate:
https://www.youtube.com/watch?v=t6m49vNjEGs
Investing helps the economy: https://www.youtube.com/watch?v=W6ICRTqsxk8

#Filler: Honey, my book can play music.
https://www.youtube.com/watch?v=HxGT5z6d-GA&list=PLMZa6mP7jZ2b1otqG4tfbgZpLEdh6YiNF

www.ingramcontent.com/pod-product-compliance
Lightning Source LLC
Chambersburg PA
CBHW051706170526
45167CB00002B/557